C000001503

FORTRESS • 89

THE ATLANTIC WALL (2)

Belgium, The Netherlands, Denmark and Norway

STEVEN J ZALOGA   ILLUSTRATED BY ADAM HOOK

Series editors Marcus Cowper and Nikolai Bogdanovic

First published in 2009 by Osprey Publishing
Midland House, West Way, Botley, Oxford OX2 0PH, UK
443 Park Avenue South, New York, NY 10016, USA
E-mail: info@ospreypublishing.com

ISBN: 978-1-84603-393-3
E-book ISBN: 978-1-84908-125-2

Editorial by Ilios Publishing Ltd, Oxford, UK (www.iliospublishing.com)
Cartography: Map Studio, Romsey, UK
Page layout by Ken Vail Graphic Design, Cambridge, UK (kvgd.com)
Typeset in Myriad and Sabon
Index by Michael Forder
Originated by PPS Grasmere
Printed in China through Bookbuilders

09 10 11 12 13   10 9 8 7 6 5 4 3 2 1

A CIP catalog record for this book is available from the British Library.

AUTHOR'S NOTE

The author would like to thank Alain Chazette for the use of photos from his extensive archive. Rob Plas and Marc van Etten provided indispensable help in helping to track down bunkers in the Hoek van Holland area. Thanks also go to Wachtmeester Alex van Riezen and to the Nederlands Instituut voor Militaire Historie for help in obtaining photos and other information on the coastal bunkers taking part in the Walcheren battles. David Keough at the US Army's Military History Institute was also most helpful in pointing out resources for this study.

ARTIST'S NOTE

THE FORTRESS STUDY GROUP (FSG)

The object of the FSG is to advance the education of the public in the study of all aspects of fortifications and their armaments, especially works constructed to mount or resist artillery. The FSG holds an annual conference in September over a long weekend with visits and evening lectures, an annual tour abroad lasting about eight days, and an annual Members' Day.

The FSG journal FORT is published annually, and its newsletter Casemate is published three times a year. Membership is international. For further details, please contact:

The Secretary, c/o 6 Lanark Place, London W9 1BS, UK

Website: www.fsgfort.com

THE WOODLAND TRUST

Osprey Publishing are supporting the Woodland Trust, the UK's leading woodland conservation charity, by funding the dedication of trees.

FOR A CATALOG OF ALL BOOKS PUBLISHED BY OSPREY MILITARY AND AVIATION PLEASE CONTACT:

Osprey Direct, c/o Random House Distribution Center, 400 Hahn Road, Westminster, MD 21157
E-mail: uscustomerservice@ospreypublishing.com

Osprey Direct, The Book Service Ltd, Distribution Centre, Colchester Road, Frating Green, Essex, CO7 7DW
E-mail: customerservice@ospreypublishing.com

www.ospreypublishing.com

CONTENTS

THE ATLANTIC WALL (2)
BELGIUM, THE NETHERLANDS, DENMARK AND NORWAY

INTRODUCTION

The Atlantic Wall was the largest and most extensive fortification program in modern European history, far outstripping the Maginot Line in length, material, and cost. This is the second book in this series, following Fortress 63 on the *Atlantikwall* on the French Atlantic coast. This volume extends the coverage from the Belgian coast eastward to the Netherlands and Denmark, and north to Norway. The previous book focused on the Atlantic Wall's primary role in repulsing the inevitable Allied invasion of France. In the case of the countries covered in this volume, the mission was more complex. Coastal defenses in Belgium were the same as those in neighboring France and part of the same anti-invasion scheme. But for the rest of this region, the *Atlantikwall* was a response to more diverse threats posed by the Royal Navy. The British art of war had long favored coastal raiding; the names of many of the fortified sites mentioned in this book elicit echoes of past battles from the Napoleonic age and before. To avoid repeating the same subjects covered in the earlier Fortress volume, this book shifts the focus away from anti-invasion defenses such as coastal obstacles, and provides greater coverage to other coastal defenses such as radar, controlled mines, and coastal defense small craft.

Norway was the first country to see extensive deployment of coastal artillery, provoked in large measure by early British commando raids. Allied deception operations through the war attempted to convince the Germans that an invasion of Norway was part of Allied strategy, in hopes of tying down German forces. There was a revival of Norwegian defenses in the late summer of 1944. The loss of critical U-boat bases in France forced the Kriegsmarine to deploy its surviving force to Norwegian harbors such as Trondheim, invigorating Royal Navy actions to these northern waters and provoking renewed defense efforts. When the Red Army pushed the Wehrmacht out of Finland via the arctic Finnmark region of Norway, coastal defenses were reinforced to protect the troop convoys streaming down along the coast from arctic waters.

Although the threat of amphibious invasion on the Dutch coast was slight due to the terrain, the important ports of Rotterdam and Amsterdam and their access to the key rivers leading into the German industrial heartland guaranteed serious fortification efforts. Denmark presents a different case altogether, with its defenses oriented primarily to keeping the British fleet out of the Baltic, with strong gun positions to cover the narrow straits.

Of the regions covered in this book, only the Netherlands saw extensive combat. The *Atlantikwall* along the Dutch coast became involved in the autumn 1944 fighting to open the approaches to Antwerp. The fiercest of these battles took place on Walcheren, where British amphibious forces paid a heavy price to overcome a concentration of fortified guns. Norway remained a backwater for most of the war, the arctic north seeing some combat in the autumn of 1944 during the withdrawal of German forces from Finland. Denmark was spared any extensive land combat and its *Atlantikwall* defenses were never tested. Curiously, Norway and Denmark became models for the final evolution of German coastal defense doctrine, serving as the proving grounds for several new types of weapon including guided torpedoes, underwater acoustic sensors, and infrared detectors.

DESIGN AND DEVELOPMENT

German coastal defenses on the North Sea date back many centuries, and during the reforms of Kaiser Wilhelm in the late 1880s, the Kriegsmarine (navy) was assigned this mission. These fortifications were modernized during World War I, and the Kriegsmarine was confronted with the need to defend the occupied Belgian coast against British naval operations. German coastal fortification in World War I was not particularly elaborate, usually consisting of open "kettle" positions (*Kesselbettungen*), which were large circular gun pits with crew shelters and protected recesses for ammunition and crew. The defense of the Belgian coast in 1914–18 helped to shape German attitudes about coastal defense when dealing with the Royal Navy. British strategy favored peripheral operations and raiding, especially against vital ports and other coastal objectives. The classic example was the British naval raid against Zeebrugge and Ostend on April 23, 1918, which attempted to sabotage both ports by sinking blockships in key passages. The Zeebrugge raid was partly successful but the German coastal batteries inflicted frightfully high casualties

on the raiding force. The Ostend raid was a failure due to German gunfire, and a repeat raid on May 10 was only marginally successful. The defense of these two ports helped establish the mission for the Kriegsmarine coastal artillery. German doctrine did not favor defenses substantial enough to prevent a full-scale invasion, but rather sufficient to deter Royal Navy raids and discourage British warships from bombarding the coast.

With the rise to power of Hitler and the Nazis in the early 1930s, Germany embarked on its most elaborate fortification effort of the modern era, the Westwall, better known to the Allies as the Siegfried Line. This linear defensive line along Germany's western frontier had little tactical relevance to the coastal defense mission, but it had a substantial technical impact on the later *Atlantikwall* in two major respects. To begin with, it helped usher in a new generation of fortress design that placed greater emphasis on shellproof and bombproof construction through the use of steel-reinforced concrete. Unlike the Maginot Line, these border fortifications were relatively small bunkers based on the experiences of the army in the trench fighting of 1917–18. Secondly, the Westwall gave added importance to Organization Todt, a paramilitary construction formation under Dr. Fritz Todt that became associated with all major German state civil engineering projects including the autobahn. Given the peculiar political dynamics of Nazi Germany with many large state organizations vying for the favor of the Führer, Organization Todt had substantial bureaucratic incentives to push grandiose construction projects whether warranted by military necessity or not. Hitler was especially susceptible to Todt's blandishments due to his personal enthusiasm for grandiose architecture, as well as his personal experience as an infantryman in the trenches in World War I where bunkers were a matter of life or death.

The blitzkrieg victories in the spring and early summer of 1940 presented the Wehrmacht with a substantial new challenge of defending an extended coastline from the Arctic Circle of northern Norway, down the Atlantic coast to the North Sea towards the Skagerrak, some 3,800km (2,400 miles). The four occupied countries in the northern sector – Norway, Denmark, Belgium, and the Netherlands – already had modest coastal artillery defenses. The only coastal defenses that played a role in the 1940 campaign were the Norwegian defenses in the Oslo Fjord where the German cruiser *Blücher* was sunk on April 9, 1940 in a duel with two fortified batteries. As the Wehrmacht deployed for occupation duties, these existing coastal defenses formed a thin crust for what would later emerge as the *Atlantikwall*.

"Alarm!" A German rifle section scrambles from a Bauform 502 personnel bunker, part of Strongpoint Roon in Middelkerke, Belgium. (A. Chazette)

Germany remained on the offensive in 1940–41 and paid little attention to defensive concerns. A significant number of large coastal batteries and railway guns were deployed to the Pas-de-Calais on the English Channel, but this was an offensive operation intended to provide fire support for the planned *Seelöwe* invasion of Britain. In 1941, Organization Todt began a large construction program in several French ports to create massive bombproof shelters to harbor the U-boat fleet in operations to strangle Britain by submarine blockade and commerce raiding; smaller schemes were also underway on submarine bunkers in Norway and S-boat (torpedo boat) shelters in the

Netherlands. With the gradual abandonment of plans to invade Britain and the strategic shift to the Russian front, there was some discussion in February 1941 of erecting fortifications along the Channel as an economy-of-force tactic, enabling relatively modest units to defend very long coastlines. Hitler rejected these plans, if for no other reason than it might tip his hand regarding plans to invade the Soviet Union in June 1941. The only area to receive heavy fortification was the Channel Islands, which enjoyed Hitler's special attention as the only British lands in his grasp.

The coastal defense dilemma emerged late in 1941 with the beginning of British raids along the Norwegian coast. British special forces landed on the Lofoten islands on the northern Norwegian coast on March 4, 1941 against minimal opposition. This prompted the Wehrmacht to reinforce the scant naval coastal batteries with army batteries. In March 1941, Norway was allotted 160 army coastal batteries and in June this program was extended by adding 90 batteries to western Europe and 10 to Denmark. British commando operations continued in Norway at Spitzbergen on August 17, 1941, and a return raid to the Lofoten islands on December 27, 1941. These raids, as well as similar ones on the French coast, were more a nuisance than a significant threat, but they caused some worry in Berlin. The direct result was a Führer

TOP LEFT
A variety of munition bunkers were developed to support artillery positions. This is an Fl 246 munition bunker, part of WN 82 Flak-Batterie Olmen in IJmuiden which supported the fortified 105mm flak positions on the crest of the coastal dune above. (Author's photograph)

TOP RIGHT
Tobruks, more formally designated as *Ringstände*, were the most widely use field fortification in the *Atlantikwall*. They were small, simple structures with a characteristic round opening for a machine gun or other weapon. Since they had an open roof and were built to the lower B1 standards, they were not designated "permanent" fortifications. This example was part of the IJmuiden fortification zone. (Author's photograph)

LEFT
This is a superb example of the open-kettle-style gun pits typical of the *Atlantikwall* in 1940–43, armed in this case with a war-booty Cockerill 120mm mle. 1931 Belgian field gun. This is part of the Batterie Saltzwedel neu/Tirpitz of 6./MAA.204 from 1941 until April 1944, and now preserved at the Domain Raversijde museum. (Author's photograph)

TOP LEFT

The Dieppe raid led to an intensive program to protect coastal batteries with steel-reinforced concrete casemates like this Bauform 671 armed with a 150mm C/36 destroyer gun and currently preserved as part of the Domain Raversijde museum. (Author's photograph)

TOP RIGHT

This is another example of camouflage, a Schneider 105mm mle. 1913 field gun of 4./HKAA.180 built at Thyboron, Denmark in 1943 with the Bauform 671 casemate enclosed in a false wooden structure to look like a civilian building. (NARA)

directive on December 14, 1941 that ordered the construction of a "New Westwall with as small a number as possible of permanent fixed troops." The directive recognized that German occupation forces were stretched very thinly along the coast, and that fortifications could substitute for manpower in remote areas. The priority for the fortification program was Norway, the French and Belgian Channel coast, the Dutch coast, and the German Bight, in that order. The emphasis on Norway in this early directive was a recognition that Norway presented an especially difficult defensive challenge due to its extensive coastline, as well as the importance of the coastal convoys along the Norwegian coast that were bringing vital materials to the German war industry from the mines in northern Norway. The coastal artillery positions had two principal missions: protection of German coastal shipping, and defense against enemy raids. The initial New Westwall construction was on a very small scale and focused on reinforcing the coastal artillery positions by providing select batteries with personnel bunkers for their crews along with protected ammunition bunkers.

On February 27/28, 1942, the commandos struck France again at Bruneval, spiriting away a secret German coastal radar. This prompted another Führer directive on March 23, 1942 which recognized that with the setbacks in Russia, the Atlantic coast eventually might be threatened with Anglo-American attacks. The highest priorities for fortification remained Norway and the Channel Islands. The fortification construction escalated a hundredfold from an initial 3,000 cubic meters of reinforced concrete used in October 1941 to 373,700 cubic meters in September 1942.

In spite of the surge in construction, the New Westwall program had limited resources due to the demands of the Russian front. The primary focus of the construction was around major ports, since these were viewed as the most attractive targets for British raids. To prioritize the construction, a few dozen key ports were designated as fortified areas (*Festungsbereichen*). The St. Nazaire raid, which occurred on March 28 only a few days after the Führer directive, only served to illustrate the continuing vulnerability of the ports. By June 1942, the New Westwall for the first time absorbed more concrete than the U-boat bunker program.

On August 13, 1942 Hitler held a meeting with senior officials to outline the strategic aim of what he now dubbed *Atlantikwall*, the Atlantic Wall. "There is only one battle front (the Russian Front). The other fronts can only be defended with modest forces... During the winter, with fanatical zeal, a fortress must be built which will hold in all circumstances...except by an attack lasting for weeks." For the first time, Hitler laid out some details of the scope of the program, indicating that the *Atlantikwall* would involve 15,000 bunkers and 300,000 troops on the Atlantic coast from Spain to the Netherlands to be finished by May 1943, the earliest time an Allied invasion of western Europe was likely. This program did not address the specific requirements for Scandinavia, though Hitler considered the projects there to be part of the overall *Atlantikwall* effort. He reiterated that the focus should be the defense of ports that were viewed as the most likely Allied objectives while the open beaches in between ports were assigned a lower priority. The August 1942 directive substantially shifted the focus of *Atlantikwall* defenses. While priority had previously gone to the Channel Islands and Norway, the focus was now shifted to the French and Belgian Channel coast. Of the 15,000 bunkers in the program, 11,000 were allocated to the AOK.7 and AOK.15 (*Armeeoberkommando*, Army high command), which covered from the western Netherlands through Belgium to Normandy. The AOK.1 on the Atlantic coast of France was allotted 1,500 to 2,000 bunkers and the remaining bunkers were authorized for the Netherlands. This shift in priority was in part due to the imminent completion of much of the fortification work on the Channel Islands, but more importantly to the growing threat of Allied invasion. Only days after this conference, the Allies struck with a massive raid at Dieppe, on August 17, 1942. The Dieppe raid only served to reinforce the urgency of the program, though it did not lead to any major change in its scope. Its one technical effect was to focus the need for better protection of the coastal artillery batteries that were vulnerable in open gun pits. The August directive led to the first major wave of *Atlantikwall* construction, the *Winterbauprogramm* (Winter Construction Program) from September 1942 through April 1943. Although the focus remained on reinforcing the numerous coastal batteries already deployed along the coast, the Dieppe raid emphasized the need to shield the gun batteries with infantry positions and to establish defenses along the so-called *Freie Küste* (open coast), the coastal areas between the ports and other defensive zones. Hitler drew the conclusion that the gun batteries had to be encased in steel-reinforced concrete, and insisted that he preferred "20 protected guns to 200 unprotected guns." This initiated the *Schartenbauprogramm* in the spring of 1943.

The *Atlantikwall* construction program relied on standardized bunker designs prepared by the army's Fortification Engineer Corps in Berlin. The original Westwall fortifications had been designated in the OB (*Offene Bettung*, open platform) or Vf (*Verstarkfeldmässig*, reinforced field position) series. Although some of these designations were retained during the construction of the Atlantic Wall, a new series of designations emerged. There is some disparity in how these designs are identified, so, for example, the "611" bunker design is variously called Bauform 611 (construction plan 611); R611 (Regelbau 611:

Some units showed considerable ingenuity in camouflaging bunkers like this example painted to resemble a house in Ostend. (National Archives Canada PA-1744386)

construction standard 611) or H611 (Heer 611: Army 611) to distinguish army bunkers from air force (L: Luftwaffe) and navy (M: Kriegsmarine) bunker designs. There were about 700 of these standard designs, of which about 250 were used on the Atlantic Wall; most of the new designs intended for the *Atlantikwall* were in the new 600 series. It should be mentioned that these designs were often modified in the field to better match local terrain contours. Besides the standardized designs, there were localized variations of standard plans as well as entirely new designs, sometimes identified with an SK suffix for *Sonderkonstruktion* (special design).

In general, Organization Todt distinguished between two main categories of fortification: the permanent (*ständige*) "bombproof" bunkers, which were fully enclosed types, and reinforced field fortifications, which were usually open-topped and included such types as open gunpits and the ubiquitous Tobruk. The latter was a small defensive position named after improvised defenses during the fighting around Tobruk in 1942 that had been created using concrete drainage pipes. Officially called *Ringstände*, the Tobruks were typically used as weapons stands fitted with an open ring position at one end. Most were built for use as machine-gun positions, but they were armed with a variety of weapons including mortars, pedestal-mounted guns and obsolete tank turrets (*Panzerstellungen*).

There were five main types of permanent, bombproof bunkers. The most common was the *Unterstand* (bunker) which came in three main varieties: the personnel bunker (*Unterstand für Mannschaften*), munitions storage bunker (*Unterstand für Munition*) and the relatively uncommon weapons garage (*Unterstand für Waffen und Gerät*). These bunkers made up more than half of all the permanent bunkers. The utility bunkers (*Versorgungsstände*) were very similar in design and included medical, kitchen and other miscellaneous types. The second most common type of permanent bunker was the gun casemate (*Schartenstand*), which was a fully enclosed gun bunker with an open embrasure and these made up about a third of the permanent bunkers on the *Atlantikwall* with widespread construction beginning in the spring of 1943. These were supported by dedicated fire-control/observation bunkers (*Beobachtungsstände*).

Table 1: *Atlantikwall* bunker construction

Region	AOK.15	AOK.7	AOK.1	Netherlands	Denmark	Norway	Total
Personnel	946	960	554	357	814		3,631
Storage	396	181	149	114	184	213	1,237
HQ	118	68	42	39	95	24	386
Gun casemate	767	876	733	241	432	131	3,180
Observation	54	34	46	6	88	43	271
Utility	72	57	42	13	140	24	348
Tobruks	2,399	3,142	1,338	1,596	?	?	
Total	*4,752*	*5,318*	*2,904*	*2,366*	*1,753*	*435*	*17,528*
Coastline (km)	708	1,566	818	383	7,314	2,532	13,321
Density/km	6.7	3.4	3.5	6.1	>0.24	>0.17	1.3

Atlantikwall fortifications on the North Sea

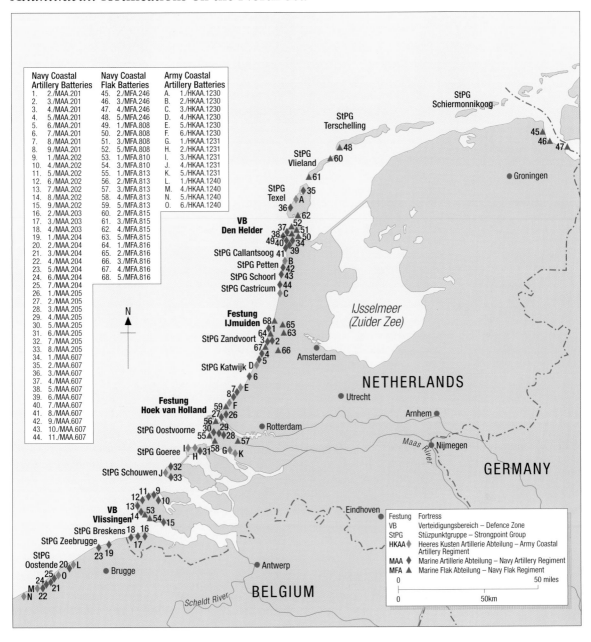

Navy Coastal Artillery Batteries		Navy Coastal Flak Batteries		Army Coastal Artillery Batteries	
1.	2./MAA.201	45.	2./MFA.246	A.	1./HKAA.1230
2.	3./MAA.201	46.	3./MFA.246	B.	2./HKAA.1230
3.	4./MAA.201	47.	4./MFA.246	C.	3./HKAA.1230
4.	5./MAA.201	48.	5./MFA.246	D.	4./HKAA.1230
5.	6./MAA.201	49.	1./MFA.808	E.	5./HKAA.1230
6.	7./MAA.201	50.	2./MFA.808	F.	6./HKAA.1230
7.	8./MAA.201	51.	3./MFA.808	G.	1./HKAA.1231
8.	9./MAA.201	52.	5./MFA.808	H.	2./HKAA.1231
9.	1./MAA.202	53.	1./MFA.810	I.	3./HKAA.1231
10.	4./MAA.202	54.	3./MFA.810	J.	4./HKAA.1231
11.	5./MAA.202	55.	1./MFA.813	K.	5./HKAA.1231
12.	6./MAA.202	56.	2./MFA.813	L.	1./HKAA.1240
13.	7./MAA.202	57.	3./MFA.813	M.	4./HKAA.1240
14.	8./MAA.202	58.	4./MFA.813	N.	5./HKAA.1240
15.	9./MAA.202	59.	5./MFA.813	O.	6./HKAA.1240
16.	2./MAA.203	60.	2./MFA.815		
17.	3./MAA.203	61.	3./MFA.815		
18.	4./MAA.203	62.	4./MFA.815		
19.	1./MAA.204	63.	5./MFA.815		
20.	2./MAA.204	64.	1./MFA.816		
21.	3./MAA.204	65.	2./MFA.816		
22.	4./MAA.204	66.	3./MFA.816		
23.	5./MAA.204	67.	4./MFA.816		
24.	6./MAA.204	68.	5./MFA.816		
25.	7./MAA.204				
26.	1./MAA.205				
27.	2./MAA.205				
28.	3./MAA.205				
29.	4./MAA.205				
30.	5./MAA.205				
31.	6./MAA.205				
32.	7./MAA.205				
33.	8./MAA.205				
34.	1./MAA.607				
35.	2./MAA.607				
36.	3./MAA.607				
37.	4./MAA.607				
38.	5./MAA.607				
39.	6./MAA.607				
40.	7./MAA.607				
41.	8./MAA.607				
42.	9./MAA.607				
43.	10./MAA.607				
44.	11./MAA.607				

Festung	Fortress
VB	Verteidigungsbereich – Defence Zone
StPG	Stüzpunktgruppe – Strongpoint Group
HKAA ◆	Heeres Kusten Artillerie Abteilung – Army Coastal Artillery Regiment
MAA ◆	Marine Artillerie Abteilung – Navy Artillery Regiment
MFA ▲	Marine Flak Abteilung – Navy Flak Regiment

The remaining types included a variety of headquarters bunkers such as command posts (*Gefechtsstände*), and radio posts (*Nachrichtenstände*). Table 1 summarizes the main types of permanent bunkers built along the *Atlantikwall* by these categories. The AOK.15 sector, which stretched from the Pas-de-Calais in France along the Belgian coast and up to the Scheldt Estuary in the Netherlands, had by far the greatest density of permanent bunkers. The Netherlands also had a relatively dense allotment of bunkers, followed by the remaining areas of the French coast, AOK.7 in Normandy and AOK.1 on the Atlantic coast and Bay of Biscay. Both Denmark and Norway had relatively thin bunker coverage; details are lacking on the total number of Tobruks built in these countries, but even if these numbers were included, the overall total number of bunkers relative to the coastline would be small compared with the other areas of the *Atlantikwall*. The Norwegian figures do not include the numerous fortifications created along the coast either by tunneling into the rock or using quarried rock for construction.

Defense sectors

Infantry defenses along the *Atlantikwall* tended to be thickest where the likelihood of invasion was greatest, so coastal infantry positions were densest in Belgium and the Netherlands, while relatively thin in Denmark and Norway. The basic tactical element of the infantry coastal defenses was the resistance nest (W or WN: *Widerstandsnest*) which usually consisted of a small number of bunkers and Tobruks, roughly between a squad and platoon in size. In important sectors, a resistance nest would be built around a gun position, such as a 50mm pedestal-mounted anti-aircraft gun in an open Tobruk, or a similar weapon in a full gun casemate. Several resistance nests formed a strongpoint (St.P.: *Stützpunkt*) which was a platoon-sized defense at minimum, and sometimes up to a company in size. Several strongpoints formed a strongpoint group (St.P.Gr.: *Stützpunktgruppe*) which was between a company and a battalion in size assigned a frontage of a kilometer or more. Several strongpoint groups formed a defense zone (VB: *Verteidigungsbereich*) though this category was not widely used in France or Belgium, which instead designated the regimental sectors as coastal defense groups (KVG: *Küsten Verteidigung Gruppen*), and the divisional sectors as coast defense sectors (KVA: *Küsten Verteidigung Abschnitte*).

The largest and most powerful coastal defense sector was the fortress (*Festung*), which was not applied to tactical field formations, but rather was reserved for strategically important sites such as major ports. The *Festung* designation encompassed all defensive formations in the defended area, and as often as not was primarily composed of Kriegsmarine formations reinforced by Heer (army) formations. A *Festung* was typically centered around a core position (*Kernwerk*), which was a heavily fortified strongpoint. The *Kernwerk* controlled the key element in the defense of the site, such as the shoulders of a port or an island covering a river estuary.

Coastal defenses in the Low Countries often included an additional seawall to prevent Allied tanks from exiting the beach. This is a fairly typical example along the beach north of Nieuport. (National Archives Canada PA-174344)

Coastal artillery

The centerpiece of German coastal defense was coastal artillery. Although there had been some design of specific coastal artillery weapons prior to 1940, the enormous demands of the *Atlantikwall* as well as its relatively low priority in German industrial planning meant that nearly all coastal artillery was adapted from naval or field artillery. In general, the Kriegsmarine established the initial port defenses and these positions were later amplified by the deployment of army coastal batteries. However, the pattern varied both by region and time, and these issues are examined in more detail in the country sections of this book.

The interior of a Bauform 612 gun casemate armed with a 75mm PaK 40 anti-tank. This bunker is part of the Domain Raversijde in Ostend, and the gun is located further back in the casemate than in wartime since the embrasure is covered to protect the interior from the weather. (Author's photograph)

Neither the army nor navy could agree on coastal artillery doctrine or tactical practices. The navy regarded their coastal artillery as a land-based version of warship artillery and followed similar fire-control practices. Kriegsmarine coastal artillery batteries were nearly always placed near the shore with direct view to sea so that the guns could engage enemy warships by direct sighting if necessary. Naval tactical doctrine stressed the need to engage moving enemy warships, so naval fire-control stations assigned to each battery had range finders and plotting tables to detect, track, and target enemy warships and to pass this data to the batteries. Besides the essential fire control post (*Leitstand*), the naval batteries often had a separate angle-measuring post (*Peilstand*) located some distance from the main battery to ensure greater precision of range-finding. The navy preferred to mount their guns on fixed, traversing mounts, which in practice meant shielded medium guns and shielded or turreted heavy guns on sockets. In practice, the navy was sometimes obliged to use field guns due to shortages of suitable naval guns.

The Batterie Saltzwedel neu/Tirpitz of 6./MAA.204 on the western side of Ostend was armed with pintle-mounted 105mm SKC/32U submarine guns in Bauform 671 casemates starting in April 1944. This well-preserved example is part of the Domain Raversijde museum; the embrasure is covered by a window to protect it from the weather. (Author's photograph)

Rheinmetall 150mm C/36 destroyer gun in coastal mounting

The army preferred to locate its coastal batteries some distance from shore so that the batteries were not immediately evident to enemy warship guns. The army saw its main mission as repel invasions or raiding parties, and engaging moving enemy warships was not a high priority. The army did not like fixed artillery for coastal defense, but preferred normal field guns. This was based on the experiences of World War I, such as those at Gallipoli, where the army drew the conclusion that it would be impossible to protect an extended shoreline with sufficient weapons, and instead opted to keep the coastal artillery mobile so that it could be moved to a threatened sector once the situation became clearer. This proved to be a very short-sighted tactical notion; Allied World War II amphibious landings had also taken the Gallipoli lessons to heart and favored brief, violent, and overwhelming attacks that would not allow the Wehrmacht time to bring up additional artillery to repel the landings. In the event, army tactical doctrine resulted in battery fire-control configurations that placed little emphasis on moving target plotting, and thus had little capability to engage moving targets beyond ordinary direct sight engagement. A Swedish coastal artillery survey of German practices after the war strongly favored the Kriegsmarine practices over the Heer's doctrine.

A quick source of coastal defenses came from the use of war-booty tank turrets like this APX-2B turret from Belgian army ACG-1 cavalry tanks. A total of 13 of these were used along the Belgian coast, this one at Ostend. (A. Chazette)

Coastal obstacles

The Wehrmacht used various types of coastal obstacle to impede the Allied use of landing craft. This program was a particular favorite of Erwin Rommel when he took over the invasion front in the autumn of 1943. These obstacles were especially dense in Belgium and the Netherlands, but quite sparse in Norway. They are covered in more detail in the previous book in this series on the Atlantic Wall in France (Fortress 63).

Coastal artillery radar

Until World War II, coastal artillery was more effective in daylight hours. Night engagements depended on illumination of the target with flares or

---

A   **RHEINMETALL 150MM C/36 DESTROYER GUN IN COASTAL MOUNTING**

One of the most common naval guns used in Kriegsmarine *Atlantikwall* gun batteries was the 15cm Torpedoboots Kanone (Tbts K) C/36. This destroyer gun had been developed by Rheinmetall in the early 1930s, and these weapons were usually deployed in the normal Tbts LC/36 mount which employed a conventional armor splinter-shield covering all of the gun except the rear. The gun and mount weighed 18.8 metric tons and employed a conventional socket which

had a special adaptor to bolt it to the floor of the casemate. The gun fired a 45.3kg projectile to a maximum range of 23.5km.

The M272 was part of a family of similar gun casemates (*Geschützschartenstände*), and the first was built in April 1943 with 27 being constructed in Norway (5), Denmark (10), Netherlands (4) and France (8). This weapon was also mounted in other types of gun casemates, such as the Bauform 671.

searchlights. These traditional techniques were far from satisfactory in the event of strong winds, fog or other weather conditions that were a frequent occurrence along the coast. The advent of naval surface-search radar opened up the possibility of creating all-weather, 24-hour coastal defenses. The Kriegsmarine had been the pioneers of German military radar and had begun to receive the Freya early warning radar in 1938; about a hundred were completed prior to the outbreak of the war, but many were requisitioned by the Luftwaffe for air defense.

Freya was followed shortly afterwards by the Seetakt (sea-tactical) radars, which were the first dedicated surface-search naval radars. The Luftwaffe sponsored a separate development track, and the Würzburg family of fire-control radars for directing flak batteries was ready in 1940. After a promising start, German radar development stagnated until 1943 due to 1941 decisions to cut long-term advanced research on the presumption that the war would soon be over. The history of German wartime radar development is too complicated to chart here, but the program had several effects on German coastal defenses. Surface search radars such as Seetakt proved to be well suited

LEFT

The most common Kriegsmarine coastal radar on the *Atlantikwall* was the FuMO-215 Würzburg-Reise, which was used both in the tactical search role, and in some cases as a dedicated artillery fire control radar. (NARA)

RIGHT

The FuMO-11 Renner was the Kreigsmarine's first attempt at a dedicated microwave artillery fire control radar, but technical problems with the design severely curtailed its deployment. (NARA)

to the early warning role and could provide good, all-weather coverage out to the horizon of enemy shipping, as long as the Allies were not employing electronic jamming. The Kriegsmarine created a Naval Tactical Radar Service and erected a chain of coastal radars as part of the *Atlantikwall* effort. By 1942, these early radars allowed German coastal artillery to engage British shipping in the Channel. These surface-search radars were not accurate enough in azimuth even if reasonably accurate in range, and this led to further interest in dedicated fire-control radars.

The small number of naval radars available did not permit each gun battery or even each regiment to have its own station. The Kriegsmarine established OZ (*Ortungszentralen*: naval radar reporting centers) as the link between the radar stations and the various other elements of coast defense. Air data was exchanged with the Luftwaffe's FMZ (*Flugmelderzentralen*: aircraft reporting centers) while naval data

Another source of electronic early warning of approaching Allied ships and aircraft were passive radar monitoring posts like this FuMB.21/27. These picked up the emissions from Allied radars and this data was used to alert the coastal radars. (NARA)

was passed to the regional Seeko. The Seeko regional command centers had an artillery staff and this staff in turn passed the data down to the artillery group commanders and then on down to the individual gun batteries by telephone. This was not an especially efficient method for fast-moving engagements and led to interest in the construction of small, inexpensive radar stations that could be deployed at the battery level.

Development of tactical artillery fire-direction radars was not mature in Germany in 1944–45. Germany attempted to adapt Allied microwave technology to the Seetakt with the centimetric FuMO-11 (Renner) radar for more precise azimuth data. However, the Renner suffered serious reliability problems and was never produced in adequate quantities. In the absence of this compact fire-control radar, the Kriegsmarine was obliged to rely on the large FuMO-214 Würzburg-Riese (Giant Würzburg), an excellent all-purpose radar originally designed for aircraft detection and flak control. These were deployed by the Kriegsmarine in the coastal role both for surface search and artillery fire direction, but the size of the radar meant that they could only be employed from large fixed sites, and were very vulnerable to Allied attack. A derivative of the FuMO-214 codenamed FuMO-214/-215 Scheer was also developed specifically for artillery fire direction and it offered better narrow-beam accuracy and greater resistance to jamming; it was never available in adequate numbers. A third fire-control radar, the Barbara, was also in development but not widely deployed.

The deployment patterns of Kriegsmarine coastal radars varied considerably from country to country. In the Netherlands, the 41st Radar Company deployed 32 naval surveillance radars, with only one at Langerak dedicated to artillery fire control and none in the air search role. In contrast, of the 41 coastal radars in Norway, 22 were used for naval surveillance, 10 as dedicated fire control radars, and 9 as air search radars. The significant difference in allotment was due in part to the large number of Luftwaffe air search radars in Netherlands as part

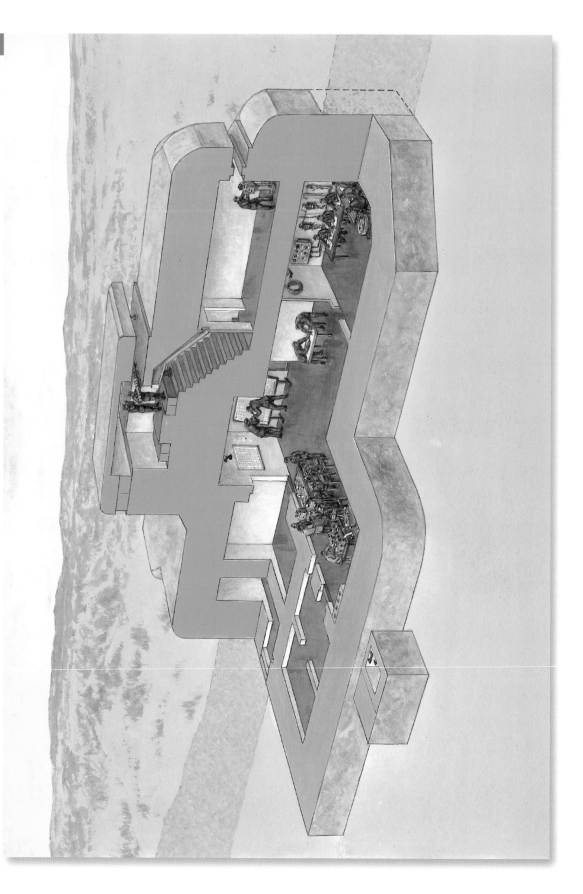

M178 fire control post, Seezielbatterie Heerenduin, WN 81, IJmuiden, The Netherlands

of the Kammhuber line shielding Germany, and the corresponding lack of need for naval air search radars. The large number of naval surveillance radars in the Netherlands along such a short coastline reduced the need for dedicated fire-control radars. Instead, the 41st Radar Company deployed two intermediate OMZ forward radar reporting stations at 's-Gravenhage (The Hague) and Den Helder besides the OZ reporting center in Haarlem to more quickly disseminate tracking data. In contrast, the gun batteries in Norway lacked nearby surveillance radars and so some of the more important batteries were issued their own FuMO-214 radar. These disparities could be seen in passive radar monitoring posts as well with nine posts in the Netherlands and only two in all of Norway.

In general, German coastal defenses had adequate coastal radar coverage for normal surveillance, but the networks seldom had the resources to provide much in the way of fire-control direction due to a shortage of microwave sets. Priority in advanced radars went to the Luftwaffe's air defense of the Reich. Furthermore, the German naval radar networks seldom had the resources or resiliency to survive dedicated Allied anti-radar campaigns that preceded major amphibious operations. The German radars could be smashed by air attack and blinded by electronic countermeasures; Anglo-American radar technology remained years ahead of German technology both in terms of the radars and electronic countermeasures.

To make up for the shortage of radars, the Kriegsmarine attempted to develop a variety of other sensors for coastal defense. The most important of these were radar interception/direction-finding receivers (*Funkmeßbeobachtungsgerät*) such as the FuMB-4 Samos and FuMB-5 Fano, which picked up the signals from Allied aircraft and ship radars. These stations could often detect Allied ships at twice the distance of neighboring radars. However, they were not precise enough for use in fire direction, and were mainly used for early warning. Allied electronic discipline during major amphibious operations dramatically reduced their effectiveness, since they had no value if the Allied ships and aircraft were not emitting signals.

Another passive target detection system was the Zeiss WPG-ZSt *Wärmepeilgerät* infrared detector. This was a forerunner of the contemporary thermal imaging fire-control system and was intended to detect enemy ships by the heat signature. This set was compact enough for use in coastal artillery

---

B   M178 FIRE CONTROL POST, SEEZIELBATTERIE HEERENDUIN, WN 81, IJMUIDEN, THE NETHERLANDS

Kriegsmarine coastal gun batteries included a fire control post (*Leitstand*) to identify, track, and designate targets for the battery. Three-story posts like this one had a rangefinder post on the top, an observation deck in the front, and working space on the lower level. The rangefinder post could use a variety of stereoscopic range finders, usually warship types mounted on sockets. The observation deck had variety of fixed observation devices for target tracking, usually a pedestal-mounted optical sight for determining bearing with the data passed electrically to the computing room below.

Although the two observation decks were the most obvious features of such a bunker, the heart of the operation was in the chambers located at the base of the bunker. These compartments mimicked the fire control on a warship, but due to the fixed position of the battery, the firing computations were less elaborate than on a moving warship. The computing

room received data from the observation decks above which were entered into the fire direction computer (*Rechenschieber*) and then integrated with bearing data from an adjacent bearing computer (*Kleingerät*) obtained from the battery's small *Peilstand* bunker located some distance away. The adjacent plotting room maintained data on the targets, usually with range and deflection plotting boards. Once the target's range, bearing, and speed were determined, a firing solution was computed and passed to the individual guns via a special switchboard (*Schaltkasten*). The fire control bunker was the battery's communication hub having radio and telephone links to higher headquarters as well as to other battery posts.

The M178 configuration shown here was first constructed in April 1943 and was not especially common, with one each in Norway and the Netherlands and two in France. However, the general features were fairly typical.

batteries, had an azimuth accuracy of two mils and could detect large warships to a range of about 15–20 kilometers. Like many devices on the "bleeding edge of technology" it had reliability and cost issues; the army showed more enthusiasm for it than the navy. The Vara battery in Norway received a set in early 1945, and the army deployed four sets in Festung Stavanger to detect approaching landing craft. In Denmark, three sets were deployed at Esbjerg in 1945 to cover the harbor entrance and a single set was being deployed near Copenhagen at Hellerup in the spring of that year.

Controlled submarine minefields

Controlled submarine mines are one of the oldest forms of naval mine. In contrast to the more familiar form of naval mines that are armed when they are deposited at sea, controlled mines are command actuated and so remain inactive for most of their deployment. They are most commonly used for harbor defense and they are especially valuable in situations where other types of naval mines would pose too great a threat to commercial waterborne traffic. The US Army was one of the most enthusiastic proponents of controlled submarine mines and had employed them in the defense of the American coast since the 19th century. Although the Kriegsmarine employed buoyant controlled mines in World War I, during the rearmament program of the 1930s the navy high command decided against a modernized equivalent. The British raids on Dieppe on August 19, 1942 and St. Nazaire on March 28, 1943 made it quite clear that German harbor defenses were inadequate and that controlled mines could provide a useful adjunct to other means of harbor defense such as coastal artillery. The Kriegsmarine had been reluctant to plant extensive minefields blocking major ports due to the hazard they posed to normal fishing and commercial traffic as well as their own warships. The controlled minefields permitted normal active minefields to be set up around the ports, with a single clear channel covered by controlled submarine mines that could be left dormant until an attack occurred.

The Kriegsmarine was not especially enthusiastic about the use of controlled mines for harbor defense, but began deploying such weapons in 1944. This is the most common type, the RMA; the control cables that led back to the shore command post are evident in this view. (NARA)

The value of controlled submarine mines remained controversial within the Kriegsmarine, but a program was begun in 1943. Rather than develop a new mine, four existing types of seabed mines were modified as controlled mines by adding watertight fittings for cables to connect them to shore. The mines were planted on the shore bottom and connected by underwater cable to a shore control station. The control station could command-detonate the mines based on visual tracking of an enemy vessel, or based on the magnetic signature of the enemy vessel from the magnetic detector in the mine itself when the ship passed overhead. The mines could also be activated to operate in a normal, automatic mode, relying on their magnetic detector. In total, 25 harbors were fitted with 729 controlled submarine mines in 1944–45, with 12 of these ports in France. Both Denmark and the Netherlands had five ports covered, while Belgium had two and Norway only one.

One of the solutions to the threat of British midget submarines was to deploy these Rheinmetall-Borsig R300 rocket-propelled depth charge launchers to Norwegian and Danish ports in 1944–45. (NARA)

The midget submarine threat

The Royal Navy began to probe German harbor defenses in Norway with midget submarines, starting with a failed Chariot attack on the battleship *Tirpitz* in the Trondheim fjord in October 1942. This attack was followed by a partially successful attack on *Tirpitz* on September 22, 1943 by X-Craft, and a failed penetration of Bergen harbor by Welman craft in November 1943. The principal underwater defense to this point had been anti-torpedo booms and nets, which were obviously inadequate. The Kriegsmarine began to investigate techniques both for the detection of the midget submarines as well as means to attack them once detected. Unlike the Royal Navy and US Navy, which had already deployed seabed magnetic anomaly detectors, the Kriegsmarine did not use this technique for harbor defense, although such a system was under development by 1945. The Kriegsmarine did attempt to deploy acoustic sensors, the Elektroakustic KHA (*Küstenhorchanlage*) and the competing Atlas Werke KUG-5. These were passive acoustic stations that were anchored in harbors to listen for enemy submarines, usually with multiple stations to make it possible to triangulate the source of the sound. One of the KHA systems was deployed at Hornbaek in Denmark, but the acoustic systems were most widely used in Norwegian harbors, with some 10 sets deployed in 6 harbors and fjords by 1945.

Rheinmetall-Borsig had already begun work on a rocket-propelled anti-submarine depth-charge launcher, the breech-loaded, single tube 380mm Raketenwerfer 300 M43 which fired a 300kg rocket projectile with a 158kg explosive charge to a range of about 3km. A small number were sent for trials with MAA.506 at Agdenes in the Trondheim fjord in April 1944 where they were judged to be reasonably successful. They were deployed in modest numbers with coastal artillery batteries to protect harbors in Norway as well as with 2./MAA.518 in Denmark in the Esbjerg defense sector. So far as is known, they were not used in combat.

Coastal commando units

One of the most desperate innovations in German coastal defense was the creation of special naval commando units in 1944. Desultory efforts to develop miniature submarines began in 1943, spurred on both by British

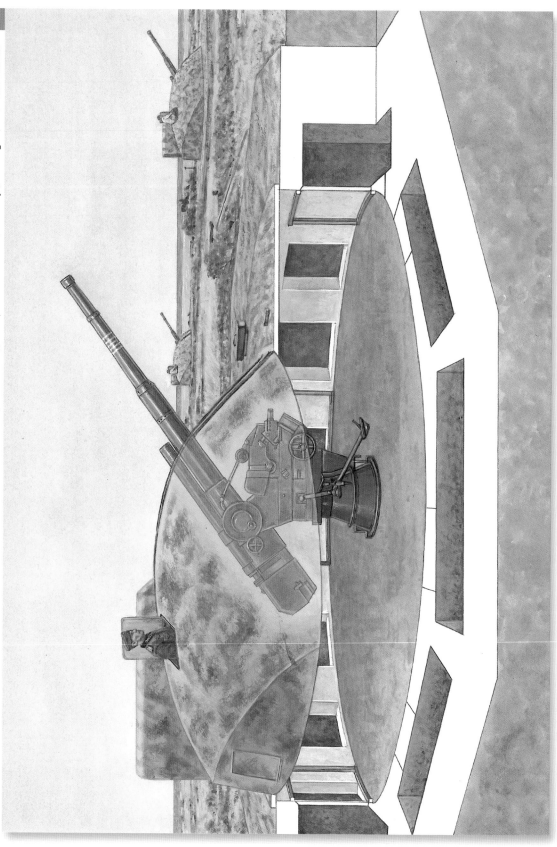

105mm SK C/32, Marine Flak Batterie West (3./MFIA.810), Stützpunkt Edelweiss, Nolledijk, Vlissingen, The Netherlands

The K-Verbände submarine units were designed to be mobile so that they could be moved to invasion sites. This Biber from K-Flotilla.261 being towed on its standard transport trailer by a half-track prime mover was burned out by an air attack on the Amiens-Bapaume road in early September 1944. (NARA)

examples and by the Italian successes in the Mediterranean. These scattered efforts were finally consolidated by Vice Admiral Helmuth Heye in April 1944 as Kommando der Kleinkampfverbände (KdK or K-Verbände: Small Combat Unit Command). The first midget submarine attacks were conducted against the Allied fleet off Anzio in late April 1944. In contrast to the Japanese, Italian and British use of small submarines, which were offensively oriented and used for naval raiding, the K-Verbände was envisioned as a novel, low-cost, anti-invasion force for coastal defense. To cut through the usual military bureaucracy, this force was independent of regional naval commands. The K-Verbände eventually took control of a wide range of unconventional weapons including manned torpedoes, midget submarines, shore-based guided torpedoes, robot attack boats, and naval commando units.

Each of the five K-Divisionen (K-Divisions) included several K-Flotilla, each specializing in a particular type of craft. The initial operations were conducted by manned torpedoes, which were an improvised submarine consisting of an unarmed, manned control torpedo on top and an armed G7e electric torpedo below. The first version, the Neger, was used at Anzio and was followed by the improved Marder. A total of six Neger/Marder flotillas were deployed; about 200 Neger and 300 Marder were built. The Marder manned torpedoes were again deployed from the French coast in July–August 1944, and were subsequently sent to Belgium, the Netherlands, Norway, and Denmark. The Marder subs were later supplemented by more sophisticated one-man

C 105MM SK C/32, MARINE FLAK BATTERIE WEST (3./MFLA.810), STÜTZPUNKT EDELWEISS, NOLLEDIJK, VLISSINGEN, THE NETHERLANDS

The 105mm SK C/32 was one of the most common Kriegsmarine flak weapons, and had originally been designed by Rheinmetall-Borsig for small warships. The basic warship version was fitted with a shrapnel shield, and this type was frequently used on land. During World War II, with the increasing use of this weapon in the coastal flak role, an enclosed turret mount was developed, primarily for weather protection, since these batteries were located along the North Sea. There were two configurations of steel cupola: the rounded type seen here, and a similar design built of welded flat sheet steel. The cupola was mounted on a variety of concrete *schwere Flakstand* gun pits with cavities for ammunition stowage around their periphery.

Each battery had four of these turrets, and this particular battery was also supported by a Fl 246 ammunition bunker; fire direction information came from a nearby Würzburg A radar codenamed Wilma. Three batteries of this regiment were located in the immediate Festung Vlissingen area, MFB Nord, Ost and West, all with the same weapons. This battery was commanded by Lt. Krautman and had a complement of 123 troops. One of its turrets was destroyed and one lightly damaged during an RAF raid on October 9. The battery saw extensive combat use both in an anti-aircraft mode and against surface targets during the fighting along the Scheldt in October 1944.

German coastal defense technology at the end of the war was a curious mix of innovation, desperation, and improvisation. There was no better example than the initial deployments of advanced, wire-guided T10 Spinne torpedoes by the K-Verbände at Strib in Denmark in early 1945. The torpedoes were housed in a concrete garage and loaded on an improvised wooden cart. To launch the torpedo, the cart was lowered to the shore by winch, and the torpedo released and launched off the cart once submerged. (NARA)

submarines which could carry two torpedoes, notably the Biber, and 10 Biber flotillas were eventually organized. About 330 Biber and 390 of the later Molch were delivered. The K-Flotillas were designed to be mobile, autonomous units that could be held in reserve away from the coast, and then rapidly moved into position by land to strike at Allied invasion forces. They were carried on a special wheeled trailer that could be rapidly moved by road using a half-track prime-mover, and then transferred into the water at a suitable boat landing or beach.

The K-Verbände also included the Linse explosive craft, which were small wooden motor boats operated in units consisting of a command boat along with two explosive boats. The explosive boats were operated by a single crewman who steered them close to the target, bailing out at an opportune moment. Control of the Linse was then taken over by radio-control from the command boat. On striking the enemy vessel, the explosive charge in the rear of the boat sank, and was detonated a few seconds after impact by a delay fuze to maximize damage. A total of 1,201 Linse boats were manufactured. A Linse flotilla had a standard complement of 16 command boats and 32 explosive boats and 11 Linse flotillas were organized. Besides the submarines and Linse boats, the K-Divisionen usually included a naval commando platoon (MEK: *Marine Einsatz Kommando*) with 30–60 troops for demolition and raiding.

The K-Verbände saw considerable combat in the Netherlands during the campaign along the Scheldt from the autumn of 1944 through the early winter of 1945, but their most extensive deployment was in Scandinavia with four of the five divisions stationed in Norway.

A TOUR OF THE SITES

Belgium

During the Great War, the Kriegsmarine's coastal artillery force experienced its first large-scale deployment away from home waters along the Belgian coast. Some 225 guns were deployed, shielding the canal exits that led to the U-boat harbor in Brugge (Bruges). The success of the U-boats in commerce raiding around Britain precipitated the legendary Royal Navy raids of March 1918 against Zeebrugge and Ostend. After the war, little of the 1918 defenses remained, having been spiked by the Germans prior to their withdrawal and scrapped after the war. Belgium had a modest array of coastal defenses in the interwar years including the excellent Vickers 94mm (3.7in.) pedestal gun, and these were initially occupied by German troops in 1940 before more elaborate defenses were organized.

The German coastal artillery forces deployed in Belgium between 1940 and 1944 were substantially less than those between 1914 and 1918. Zeebrugge lost its strategic importance, as the longer-ranged U-boats were based out of harbors in France rather than in the more confined waters of Belgium. The *Atlantikwall* in Belgium was largely an extension of the Channel defenses in the neighboring Pas-de-Calais region of France under AOK.15 control. As a result, the defense sectors here were numbered and

TOP LEFT

Kettle positions were typical of the early Belgian batteries like this camouflaged 155mm GPF of 3./HKAA.1260 in Middelkerke. (A. Chazette)

TOP RIGHT

Some of the early naval batteries in Belgium had the advantage of shielded guns like this 105mm SKL/40 of 7./MAA.204 Seezielbatterie Kursaal. (A. Chazette)

MIDDLE

Bunkers were often sheathed in camouflage nets as seen in this stretch of defenses at Wenduine near Blankenbergh in September 1944, part of a 1.Marine-Funkmessabteilung coastal radar post. A Würzburg Riese radar is evident to the right. (National Archives Canada PA-174350)

LEFT

The Belgian coast had a relatively heavy concentration of railroad guns for its heavy artillery. This is the 280mm Kurze Bruno station in Bredene with E.696. (A. Chazette)

The brains of the naval gun batteries were contained in the plotting rooms located deep inside the fire control post. These rooms contained a variety of mechanical and electro-mechanical computing devices, which converted data from the range finders and bearing devices into firing solutions for the battery's guns. (NARA)

Table 2: Wehrmacht coastal artillery batteries in Belgium, summer 1944

Navy coastal batteries	Battery name	No. of guns	Caliber
1./MAA.204	Seezielbatterie Hamilton	4	75mm
2./MAA.204	Seezielbatterie Hundius	4	105mm
3./MAA.204	Seezielbatterie Salzwedel-Alt	4	75mm
4./MAA.204	Seezielbatterie Ramien	4	105mm
5./MAA.204	Seezielbatterie Schütte	4	105mm
6./MAA.204	Seezielbatterie Salzwedel-Neu	4	105mm
7./MAA.204	Seezielbatterie Kursaal	4	105mm
Army coastal batteries	**Battery name**	**No. of guns**	**Caliber**
1./HKAA.1240	HKB Vosscheslag	6	155mm
4./HKAA.1240	HKB Groenendijk	6	155mm
5./HKAA.1240	HKB De Panne	6	155mm
6./HKAA.1240	HKB Westende	6	155mm
Army railroad batteries	**Battery location**	**No. of guns**	**Caliber**
E.718	Knokke	3	170mm
E.717	Blankenberghe	3	170mm
E.655	Zeebrugge	4	150mm
E.687	Lisseweghe	2	203mm
E.690	Bredene	4	280mm

named in the AOK.15 fashion as KVA.A (*Küsten Verteidigung Abschnitt-A*: Coast Defense Sector-A). Each KVA roughly corresponded to a divisional sector, and was further divided into three regimental sectors (KVA.A1 to A3).

The navy guns in Belgium were an unusually motley selection including Tsarist 3in. field guns rechambered by the Poles in 1926 for standard French 75mm ammunition, as well as more conventional naval guns. The predominant army coastal weapon was the K418(f), better known by its French designation of 155mm GPF. The most powerful weapons in Belgium were not the fixed batteries, but rather four railroad gun batteries. The most common weapon was the 170mm K(E), which was a gun taken from the World War I *Deutschland* class and remounted on rail carriages, and there was also a battery with the powerful 280mm Kurze Bruno. As in the neighboring AOK.15 sectors in France, the Belgian coast had a denser concentration of infantry positions than in the neighboring Netherlands because of its role in defending against an expected Allied amphibious invasion. In the summer of 1944 it was occupied by the 712.Infanterie Division, 89.Armee Korps. Since the Belgian coast was only 36 miles (58km) long, the *Atlantikwall* construction there consumed only 510,420 cubic meters of concrete – less than five percent of the total.

The Netherlands

Coastal defenses in the Netherlands constituted about a tenth of total *Atlantikwall* fortification activity in 1942–44. The Netherlands was never

ABOVE LEFT
Coastal strongpoints frequently had forward artillery observation bunkers in the dunes like this Bauform 143, part of St.P. Lohengrin in Zoutelande between Westkapelle and Vlissingen. The armored cupola can be seen on the roof on the bunker. Note also that the rear entrance door is well protected by a machine-gun position in enfilade. This particular bunker has been expertly restored by the Bunkerbehoud foundation and has a full interior; the rails on the roof are a safety feature and not part of the original design. (Author's photograph)

ABOVE RIGHT
Life in a German coastal bunker was cramped. This is the preserved interior of a Bauform 502 of St.P. Lohengrin in Vlissingen and this small room would have accommodated ten soldiers. (Author's photograph)

LEFT
Seezielbatterie Wijk-am-Zee, 2./ MAA.201, was equipped with four Bauform 671 gun casemates as seen to the right which were armed with 150mm TbKC/36 naval guns during the war. Its M473a fire control post can be seen to the left; it was in use as a seaside restaurant when visited by the author in 2008. (Author's photograph)

A "battleship of the dunes," the Seezielbatterie Schveningen-Nord of 8./MAA.201 armed with 150mm SKC/28 naval guns. In this view, the multi-tier S414 fire control post can be seen in the foreground as well as three of the Bauform 671 gun casemates beyond. (Author's photograph)

especially high on the list of probable Allied invasion points, since the low-lying land behind the coastal dikes could be readily flooded and made impassible. The Dutch ports at Rotterdam and Amsterdam and their access to key waterways leading into the German industrial heartland ensured a significant fortification effort on the Dutch coast. A secondary reason for heavy defense of the Dutch ports was their role in basing S-boat torpedo boats, which were very active in the naval campaigns in the North Sea. A number of substantial S-boat shelters were built in Dutch harbors to defend this force against RAF bomber raids.

The majority of the Dutch coastal defenses were subordinate to the WBN (*Wehrmachtsbefehl in den Niederlanden*: Armed Forces Command in the Netherlands). The exception was the Scheldt estuary region around Breskens and Vlissingen; it was subordinate to the neighboring AOK.15 which controlled German army units in the Pas-de-Calais and Belgian coast.

There were four primary defense zones in the Netherlands, two designated at the highest level as *Festung* (fortress) and the other two as *Verteidigungsbereich* (defense zone). The single most heavily fortified area was the Hoek van Holland (Hook of Holland) due to its strategic importance. Aside from including the cities of The Hague and Rotterdam, this estuary and port area offered access to the two most important rivers in this area of northern Europe, the Maas (Meuse) and the Rhine. Nearly a quarter of the major fortifications built in the Netherlands during the war were located in this sector. The defense centered around the New Waterway, the late 19th-century canal connecting Rotterdam to the North Sea. The center of the defenses was its *Kernwerk* on the south bank of the canal near the site of today's Europort.

The second *Festung* in the Netherlands was IJmuiden. While this small fishing port would hardly seem to merit such a designation, the fortified area served to cover the entrance of the neighboring North Sea Canal which led to Amsterdam and the IJsselmeer (Zuider Zee). The *Kernwerk* was based on Forteiland, a Dutch fortified island at the entrance of the canal. This *Festung* also included a heavy concentration of naval flak batteries for air defense, along with fortified radar stations.

The northernmost of the major Dutch fortified zones was VB Den Helder. This site had strategic significance as a major port at the tip of North Holland, controlling naval access into the IJsselmeer. The fourth major defense sector was VB Vlissingen (Flushing), which controlled access to the Scheldt Estuary and the port of Antwerp. This defense sector included a substantial arsenal of naval batteries facing the North Sea, as well as additional batteries to control the Scheldt. On the southern bank of the Scheldt Estuary was Strongpoint Group Breskens, a substantial defensive position in its own right with a significant *Landfront*. Although these defensive positions were originally under WBN control, in September 1942, they were transferred to the neighboring AOK.15 command as part of the Channel Coast defense effort. With the advance of Canadian and British forces in August 1944, the AOK.15 responsibility was shifted further up the coast, taking control of strongpoints up to Oostvoorne. With the liberation of Antwerp in September 1944, the Scheldt Estuary suddenly took on greater importance, since without control of the Scheldt the port was virtually useless due to the threat of the substantial German coastal defenses. Due to this change in importance, this sector was redesignated as *Festung* and played a significant role in the brutal October–November 1944 engagements which will be covered in more detail later.

Besides the usual coastal artillery batteries, the Netherlands had an unusually heavy deployment of Kriegsmarine flak batteries. These were most often dual-purpose 105mm naval guns that had a secondary role of coast defense. The widespread deployment was in part due to the need to defend Dutch harbors from RAF attacks, but the Netherlands was in the path of Allied heavy bombers heading towards Germany. So the batteries were used both in harbor defense and against the bomber streams. In 1943 alone, the naval flak batteries fired 13,253 rounds of 105mm and 26,914 rounds of 20mm ammunition. The flak batteries played an important role in defending Dutch harbors as they were available in sufficient quantity to make air attacks costly. For example, on January 17, 1945 a raid by 30 Beaufighters of 16 Group into the Den Helder anchorage led to the loss of six aircraft.

Festung harbors in the Netherlands were based around a heavily fortified *Kernwerk* at the core of the position. In the case of IJmuiden on the approaches to Amsterdam, the WN 73 *Kernwerk* was based on the previous Dutch defenses on Forteiland, a small island bisecting the channel. The brick structure in center is the original Dutch *Kustfort* built in 1880–87 and armed with Krupp 240mm guns. On either side, two of three Kriegsmarine M170 gun casemates are visible; they were armed with 150mm SKL/40(h) naval guns. One of a pair of Bauform 631 anti-tank gun casemates is visible in the lower right, largely submerged from erosion. This small island, some 680m long and 300m wide, had 26 major bunkers built on it, many of which still survive. (Author's photograph)

WN 73 Kernwerk IJmuiden, North Sea Canal, The Netherlands

Adjacent to the IJmuiden Kernwerk was WN.81, which included Seezielbatterie Heerenduin of 4./MAA.201, armed with four 170mm SKL/40 naval guns in M272 casemates. The centerpiece was this M178 naval fire control post. (Author's photograph)

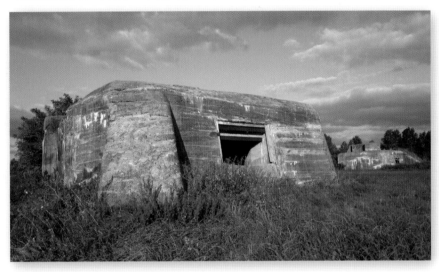

The army also deployed some of its divisional field guns in casemates like this battery on the outskirts of Bergen-op-Zoom with four Bauform 669 casemates for the batteries of Artillerie Regiment 1719 of the 719.Infanterie Division. The battery's casemates are unusual in that several had an additional Tobruk position built on top. (Author's photograph)

D WN 73 KERNWERK IJMUIDEN, NORTH SEA CANAL, THE NETHERLANDS

The *Festung* ports on the North Sea were typically based around a core position (*Kernwerk*) which covered the main port entrance – in this case, the North Sea Canal entrance into Amsterdam. The IJmuiden *Kernwerk* was built on Forteiland, a Dutch fortified island with the *Kustfort* built in 1880–87 and armed with German 240mm guns; it was modernized in the 1920s with several more modern small bunkers. The island was substantially rebuilt in the summer of 1943 while manned by 3./MAA.201. The Dutch *Kustfort* was reinforced by adding three large M170 casemates for World War I 150mm naval guns with associated personnel bunkers, plus a fire control post. These bunkers were defended by a host of smaller bunkers containing antitank guns and machine guns, and two more artillery batteries were added, armed with war-booty Soviet 122mm A-19 field guns. The seaward beach was covered with dragons' teeth to prevent the landing of tanks or vehicles.

This *Kernwerk* was part of an interlocking defense system with extensive artillery on both shoulders of the canal. Seezielbatterie Heerenduin, located on the IJmuiden coast south of the canal,

had four 170mm SKL/40 naval guns in M272 casemates, while Seezielbatterie Wijk-am-See on the north had a battery of 150mm Tsts.K C/36 guns in Bauform 671 casemates. This *Festung* was also supported by a heavy concentration of naval flak batteries for air defense along with fortified radar stations.

1.   Bauform 636 SK fire control post
2–4.   M170 gun casemates for 150mm SKL/40 gun with adjacent Bauform 656 15-man personnel bunker
5.   Bauform 671 SK gun casemate for British 3.7-inch gun
6–7.   Bauform 611 gun casemate for Soviet 122mm A-19 gun
8–13.   Bauform 631 antitank gun bunker
14–15. Bauform 633 Mortar pit
16–19. Bauform 644 machine-gun casemate
20.   Local design decontamination building
21.   Bauform 635 Double group (20-man) personnel bunker
22.   Water reservoir
23–24. Depth charge launcher
25.   Storage bunker
26.   Bauform 668 6-man bunker used as canteen

Table 3: Wehrmacht coastal artillery batteries in the Netherlands, summer 1944

Naval battery	Battery name	Casemate	No. of guns	Caliber
2./MAA.201	Seezielbatterie Wijk-am-Zee	671	4	150mm
3./MAA.201	Kernwerk IJmuiden	M170, 611	3+2	150mm
4./MAA.201	Seezielbatterie Heerenduin (Prien)	M272	4	170mm
5./MAA.201	Seezielbatterie Langerak	M153c	4	150mm
6./MAA.201	Seezielbatterie Zuidzand	M671	4	94mm
7./MAA.201	Seezielbatterie Noordwijk	671	4	155mm
8./MAA.201	Seezielbatterie Schveningen-Nord	671	4	150mm
9./MAA.201	Seezielbatterie Westduin	671	4	105mm
1./MAA.202	Seezielbatterie Dishoek		4	150mm
4./MAA.202	Seezielbatterie Oostkapelle	671	3	94mm
5./MAA.202	Seezielbatterie Domburg	612	4	220mm
6./MAA.202	Seezielbatterie Westkapelle	671	4	94mm
7./MAA.202	Seezielbatterie Zoutelande	671SK	6	155mm
8./MAA.202	Seezielbatterie Fidelio	612	4	220mm
9./MAA.202	Kernwerk Vlissingen	M170	3	150mm
2./MAA.203	Seezielbatterie Breskens	671	4	76.2mm
3./MAA.203	Seezielbatterie Nieuwe Sluis	612	4	120mm
4./MAA.203	Seezielbatterie Cadzand	671	4	150mm
1./MAA.205	Marko-Stand[1]	n/a	n/a	
2./MAA.205	Seezielbatterie Vineta	671	4	150mm
3./MAA.205	Seezielbatterie Rozenburg	S412	3	280mm
4./MAA.205	Schwere Seezielbatterie Brandenburg	SK Bettung	3	240mm
5./MAA.205	Kernwerk Hoek van Holland	M170/622	4+2	120mm
6./MAA.205	Seezielbatterie Rockanje	671	4	94mm
7./MAA.205	Seezielbatterie Renesse Neu	671	4+3	75mm
8./MAA.205	Seezielbatterie Westerschouwen	671	6	94mm
1./MAA.607	Marko-Stand	n/a		
2./MAA.607	Seezielbatterie Eierland	M195	4	105mm
3./MAA.607	Seezielbatterie Hors	671	4	120mm
4./MAA.607	Seezielbatterie Kaaphoofd	612	4	105mm
5./MAA.607	Seezielbatterie Duinrand	no	4	194mm
6./MAA.607	Seezielbatterie Falga	671	4	120mm
7./MAA.607	Seezielbatterie Zanddijk	M219	4	120mm
8./MAA.607	Seezielbatterie Callantsoog	671	4	76.2mm
9./MAA.607	Seezielbatterie Camperduin	612/671	4	105mm
10./MAA.607	Seezielbatterie Bergen	671	4	120mm
11./MAA.607	Seezielbatterie Egmond am See	671	4	105mm

Notes

[1] Marko-Stand= Marineartilleriekommando-stand/stabsbatterie: Naval artillery command post/ staff battery

[2] HKB= Heeresküstenbatterie

[3] Flagruko= Flakgruppenkommandostand/ stabsbatterie: Flak group command post/staff battery

Army battery	Battery name	Casemate	No. of guns	Caliber
Army batteries				
1./HKAA.1230	HKB[2] De Koog		6	105mm
2./HKAA.1230	HKB Petten	612	4	105mm
3./HKAA.1230	HKB Castricum	671	4	105mm
4./HKAA.1230	HKB Hillegom	669/671	6	105mm
5./HKAA.1230	HKB Katwijk	688	6	152mm
6./HKAA.1230	HKB Monster	Bettung	6	152mm
1./HKAA.1231	HKB Helvoet		4+2	105mm
2./HKAA.1231	HKB Goedereede	671	4	105mm
3./HKAA.1231	HKB Ouddorp	669/671	6	152mm
4./HKAA.1231	HKB Haamstede	671	4	105mm
5./HKAA.1231	HKB Hellevoet	671	4	105mm

Naval Flak battery	Battery name	Casemate	No. of guns	Caliber
Naval coastal Flak batteries				
2./MFA.246	Schw.Flak-Battr. Nansum	no	4	105mm
3./MFA.246	Schw.Flak-Battr. Delfzil	no	4	105mm
4./MFA.246	Schw.Flak-Battr. Termunten	no	4	105mm
5./MFA.246	Marine-Flak-Battr. Terschelling-West	FL 243a	4	105mm
1./MFA.808	Flagruko[3] Den Helder	n/a	n/a	n/a
2./MFA.808	Marine-Flak-Battr. Dirksz-Admiral	FL 243/L 401	4	105mm
3./MFA.808	Marine-Flak-Battr. Vangdam	no	4	105mm
5./MFA.808	Marine-Flak-Battr. Erfprinz	FL243/L401	4	105mm
1./MFA.810	Flagruko Heldburg	n/a	n/a	n/a
3./MFA.810	Marine-Flak-Battr. West	no	4	105mm
1./MFA.813	Flagruko Hoek van Holland	n/a	n/a	n/a
2./MFA.813	Marine-Flak-Battr. Nordmole	no	4	105mm
3./MFA.813	Marine-Flak-Battr. Waterweg	FL243	4	105mm
4./MFA.813	Marine-Flak-Battr. Briel	FL243	4	105mm
5./MFA.813	Marine-Flak-Battr. Zande	no	4	105mm
2./MFA.815	Marine-Flak-Battr. Vlieland-Ost	FL243a	4	105mm
3./MFA.815	Marine-Flak-Battr. Vlieland-West	FL243a	4	105mm
4./MFA.815	Marine-Flak-Battr. Den Hoorn	no	4	105mm
5./MFA.815	Marine-Flak-Battr. Kreuzberg	no	4	105mm
1./MFA.816	Flagruko	n/a	n/a	n/a
2./MFA.816	Marine-Flak-Battr. Beverwijk	no	4	105mm
3./MFA.816	Marine-Flak-Battr. Süd-Ost	no	4	105mm
4./MFA.816	Marine-Flak-Battr.Olmen	FL243	6	105mm
5./MFA.816	Marine-Flak-Battr. Duinenberg	no	4	105mm

Panzerturm II (S-Behelfsausführung), Festung Lista, Norway

German fortification efforts in Norway in 1940–41 focused on the construction of massive U-boat bunkers in Trondheim. These facilities became more important in the autumn of 1944 after the loss of U-boat bases in France, leading to additional coastal defense efforts in the area. This is a view of the submarine bunkers immediately at the end of the war. (NARA)

Norway

Of the North Sea coastlines described in this book, Norway was the first to see extensive coastal defense efforts starting in 1940, and had priority over the French–Belgian coast well into 1943. The early emphasis on Norway was due to a variety of factors including the strategic importance of the ore supplies from northern Norwegian and neighboring Swedish mines and the corresponding need to protect the coastal traffic, as well as the imperative to interdict the British Arctic convoys supplying the Red Army through Murmansk. Norway also provided a means to control the northern shore of the Skagerrak and therefore access towards the Baltic and the northwestern German coast. At the same time, the Norwegian coast was all too accessible to British naval centers such as Scapa Flow, and vulnerable to raiding operations by the Royal Navy. Norway presented some unique problems and some unique potential for coastal defense.

E   **PANZERTURM II (S-BEHELFSAUSFÜHRUNG), FESTUNG LISTA, NORWAY**

Wehrmacht defensive positions in Norway made extensive use of *Panzerstellungen*, which consisted of obsolete tank turrets mounted on bunkers derived from the common Tobruk/Ringstand designs. In this case, the turrets were leftovers from the PzKpfw II (F) Flamingo flamethrower tanks, termed expedient version (*Behelfsausführung*) as they were cheaply adapted for the role by blanking off the more elaborate pivoting visors used on the tank. A coaming was added on the front turret roof to improve ventilation. A total of 63 of this version were converted by Schichau in Elbing, along with 25 of the normal series using unmodified Flamingo turrets; 31 of the expedient version seen here were sent to Norway and 4 of the normal series to Denmark; the rest went to the Eastern Front.

The Tobruk is a Bauform 232a dating from March 1943 and is fairly typical of *Panzerstellungen*, with a circular opening capped by an octagonal steel plate bolted to the roof. These bunkers were built to the reduced B1 standards of concrete thickness and so were intended to be fully buried except for whatever opening was needed for access to the interior, in this case some crude steps along the side. The interior was a simple pit under the gun and a compartment in the back for ammunition stowage; the unit of fire, the standard ammunition allotment, was 12,000 rounds. Since they were considered reinforced field positions, no armored door was provided, although some units would add an improvised wooden door for weather protection. The turrets were originally delivered in dark grey, but later in "light tropical color" (*heller Tropenanstich*, RAL 7028), which was also widely used on many other *Atlantikwall* components. Sometimes, camouflage colors were applied over this, but most photos show a single color.

The battlecruiser *Gneisenau*'s C turret was emplaced near Trondheim in MKB 1/507 near Orlandet in 1943; this image shows the battery shortly after its completion but before camouflage nets were attached. This battery remained in Norwegian service after the war and is currently preserved as a museum. (NARA)

This is a typical example of the early Norwegian coastal artillery deployments, in this case a French Schneider 105mm mle. 1913. The kettle position includes a concrete slab with pintle, on which was mounted a traversable platform. The gun was lashed to this for rapid traverse. (NARA)

The enormous length of coastline was a formidable challenge to establishing any sort of comprehensive defense line. The Norwegian coast extended from the Skagerrak to the North Cape on the Arctic Ocean, a distance of 2,532km (1,570 miles) though the actual coastline was a daunting 25,148km if measured along the numerous fjords. Much of the coast was mountainous and undeveloped which presented enormous difficulty in moving any large construction equipment into place for fortification purposes. On the other hand, the rocky coastline also permitted the construction of defensive works by digging into the rockbed to minimize the need for extensive amounts of steel-reinforced concrete.

The enormous length of the Norwegian coast forced the Wehrmacht to divide the country into three defense sectors each with a Kriegsmarine command and corresponding Heer command. The navy's sectors were Admiral der Westküste headquartered in Bergen, Admiral der Nordküste based in

Table 4: Einsatzgruppe Wiking permanent bunkers in Norway through July 1944

Bunker	Storage	HQ	Gun	Platform	Observation	Medical	Torpedo
Kirkenes	14	1	9	0	1	1	1
Alta	9	4	5	0	2	0	0
Moen	5	1	0	0	1	0	0
Narvik	14	1	2	7	2	0	0
Bodo/Mosjoen	14	0	29	0	3	1	0
Trondheim	26	9	12	1	9	6	2
Andalsnes	36	1	16	0	2	2	2
Bergen	42	3	18	1	6	4	1
Kristiansand	50	5	24	4	14	10	0
Tonsberg	3	0	3	0	3	0	0
Total	**213 (296)[1]**	**25 (30)**	**118 (220)**	**13 (20)**	**43 (71)**	**24 (44)**	**6 (9)**

Notes

[1] Numbers in parentheses indicate the number of bunkers intended for completion

Trondheim and Admiral der Polarküste in Tromso. In turn, these sectors were divided into regional sea commands (*Seekommandant/Seeko*). The Heer units were subordinate to Armeeoberkommando Norwegen (Norway Army High Command) though after January 1942, the Kirkenes sector fell under AOK Lappland (later AOK.20 Gebirgs) which was responsible for the Finnish front. At peak strength the army had five corps in Norway, including one in the Kirkenes sector not under AOK Norwegen command, but by 1945 this had been whittled down by the transfer of one corps to other fronts.

German fortification work in Norway initially began in mid-1941 with the construction of reinforced submarine bunkers in Trondheim. Organization Todt created the Einsatzgruppe Wiking to specialize in construction work in Scandinavia. Fortification efforts in the more remote northern areas were considerably hampered by the lack of road and rail lines, and prompted an ambitious German program to construct a supporting transportation network to link German occupation forces. A further incentive to create a road and rail network in the north was Hitler's scheme to create a major German port in the Trondheim area with facilities for a quarter-million German military and civilian personnel. The enormous demands of these construction schemes

BELOW LEFT
Besides French artillery, the Norwegian batteries also made extensive use of World War I artillery, such as this Skoda 210mm K39/40, originally ordered by Turkey from Czechoslovakia but kept in production after 1939. (NARA)

BELOW RIGHT
The difficulty of erecting concrete casemates in the remote regions of Norway meant that most batteries relied on camouflage umbrellas like this 240mm SKL/40 of MKB 4/517 Batterie Mestersand near Sylt in 1943. (NARA)

The *Atlantikwall* in Scandinavia, 1944–45

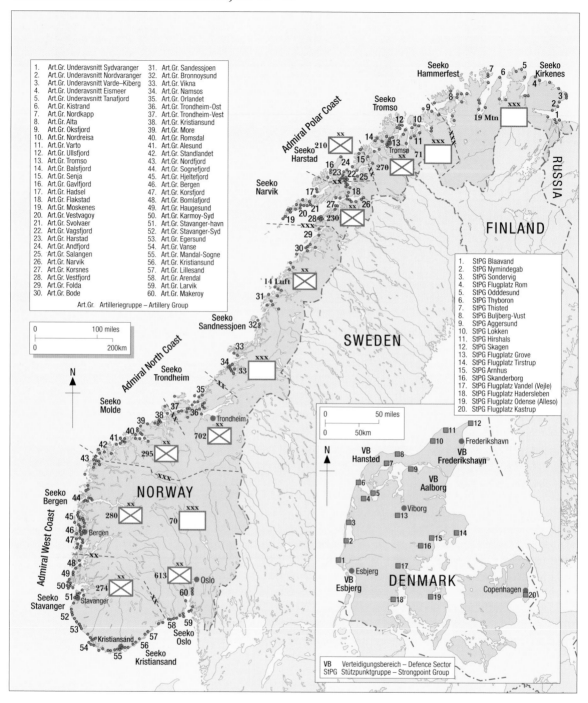

1. Art.Gr. Underavsnitt Sydvaranger
2. Art.Gr. Underavsnitt Nordvaranger
3. Art.Gr. Underavsnitt Varde–Kiberg
4. Art.Gr. Underavsnitt Eismeer
5. Art.Gr. Underavsnitt Tanafjord
6. Art.Gr. Kistrand
7. Art.Gr. Nordkapp
8. Art.Gr. Alta
9. Art.Gr. Oksfjord
10. Art.Gr. Nordreisa
11. Art.Gr. Varto
12. Art.Gr. Ullsfjord
13. Art.Gr. Tromso
14. Art.Gr. Balsfjord
15. Art.Gr. Senja
16. Art.Gr. Gavlfjord
17. Art.Gr. Hadsel
18. Art.Gr. Flakstad
19. Art.Gr. Moskenes
20. Art.Gr. Vestvagoy
21. Art.Gr. Svolvaer
22. Art.Gr. Vagsfjord
23. Art.Gr. Harstad
24. Art.Gr. Andfjord
25. Art.Gr. Salangen
26. Art.Gr. Narvik
27. Art.Gr. Korsnes
28. Art.Gr. Vestfjord
29. Art.Gr. Folda
30. Art.Gr. Bode
31. Art.Gr. Sandessjoen
32. Art.Gr. Bronnoysund
33. Art.Gr. Vikna
34. Art.Gr. Namsos
35. Art.Gr. Orlanden
36. Art.Gr. Trondheim-Ost
37. Art.Gr. Trondheim-Vest
38. Art.Gr. Kristiansund
39. Art.Gr. More
40. Art.Gr. Romsdal
41. Art.Gr. Alesund
42. Art.Gr. Standlandet
43. Art.Gr. Nordfjord
44. Art.Gr. Sognefjord
45. Art.Gr. Hjeltefjord
46. Art.Gr. Bergen
47. Art.Gr. Korsfjord
48. Art.Gr. Bomlafjord
49. Art.Gr. Haugesund
50. Art.Gr. Karmoy-Syd
51. Art.Gr. Stavanger-havn
52. Art.Gr. Stavanger-Syd
53. Art.Gr. Egersund
54. Art.Gr. Vanse
55. Art.Gr. Mandal-Sogne
56. Art.Gr. Kristiansund
57. Art.Gr. Lillesand
58. Art.Gr. Arendal
59. Art.Gr. Larvik
60. Art.Gr. Makeroy

Art.Gr. Artilleriegruppe – Artillery Group

0 100 miles
0 200km

N

1. StPG Blaavand
2. StPG Nymindegab
3. StPG Sondervig
4. StPG Flugplatz Rom
5. StPG Odddesund
6. StPG Thyboron
7. StPG Thisted
8. StPG Buljberg-Vust
9. StPG Aggersund
10. StPG Lokken
11. StPG Hirshals
12. StPG Skagen
13. StPG Flugplatz Grove
14. StPG Flugplatz Tirstrup
15. StPG Arnhus
16. StPG Skanderborg
17. StPG Flugplatz Vandel (Vejle)
18. StPG Flugplatz Hadersleben
19. StPG Flugplatz Odense (Alleso)
20. StPG Flugplatz Kastrup

0 50 miles
0 50km

N

VB Verteidigungsbereich – Defence Sector
StPG Stützpunktgruppe – Strongpoint Group

consumed most of the early supplies of reinforced concrete and slowed any coastal defense fortification. Local units were obliged to make do with improvisations, including the use of rock to create expedient defenses and to use caves and tunnels for ammunition and personnel shelters. In comparison with the *Atlantikwall* in France, Norway was very weakly provided with reinforced concrete shelters. So while there were over 2,000 gun casemates in France, there were only about a hundred in Norway.

Table 5: Artillery deployment in Norway by caliber

Caliber	Guns	Batteries
406mm	7	2
380mm	6	2
305mm	4	1
280mm	12	4
240mm	13	3
210mm	73	23
170mm	15	4
155mm	242	52
145mm	50	11
130mm	12	3
127mm	24	6
122mm	5	1
120mm	39	11
105mm	368	95
100mm	46	12
65–94mm	117	30
Total	**1,033**	**260**

The initial steps to defend the Norwegian coast began late in 1940 with Kriegsmarine plans to absorb 13 existing Norwegian coastal batteries, add additional batteries from captured Norwegian army artillery, and reinforce these batteries with additional artillery to increase the total to 44 navy coastal batteries. The difficulties of moving construction supplies to many of the more remote coastal positions forced the naval coastal batteries to deploy in open field emplacements in many locations. As a minimum, attempts were made to provide a concrete platform with pintle mount for medium coastal guns and to provide some form of protected ammunition and crew shelter. The British coastal raids in March 1941 infuriated Hitler and triggered a scheme to increase the Norwegian coastal batteries with 160 army coastal batteries.

The vast majority of coastal artillery pieces deployed to Norway were war-booty rather than standard German field artillery or naval guns; about 1,100 guns were eventually deployed in Norway. In comparison, there were

The *Gneisenau* turret of Batterie Fjell (MKB.11/504) near Bergen was covered with a camouflage umbrella typical of Norwegian sites consisting of wooden outriggers and wire netting with painted metal squares and dried brush. (NARA)

Table 6: coastal batteries, Admiral Polar Coast

Artillery group	Command unit						
Art.Gr. Underavsnitt Sydvaranger	HKAA.478	HKB 1/478	HKB 2/478	HKB 4/478	HKB 6/478	HKB 999	MKB 3/517	MKB 4/517
		4x 75mm	4x 105mm	4x 105mm	4x 105mm	4x 75mm	3x 150mm	4x 240mm
Art.Gr. Underavsnitt Nordvaranger	2./MKB.513	HKB 3/478	MKB 2/513					
		4x 105mm	3x 130mm					
Art.Gr. Underavsnitt Vardo-Kiberg	MAA.513	HKB 1/448	HKB 5/448	MKB 3/513	MKB 4/513			
		4x 105mm	3x 210mm	3x 280mm	4x 88mm			
Art.Gr. Underavsnitt Eismeer	HKAA.448	HKB 2/448	HKB 3/448	HKB 4/448				
		5x 145mm	5x 145mm	5x 155mm				
Art.Gr. Underavsnitt Tanafjord	HKAA.480	HKB 1/480	HKB 2/480	HKB 3/480	HKB 4/480	HKB 5/480	MKB 1/513	
		4x 105mm	4x 105mm	6x 145mm	6x 145mm	4x 145mm	3x 130mm	
Art.Gr. Kistrand	I./HKAA.971	HKB 4/971	HKB 5/971	HKB 6/971	HKB 7/971	HKB 31/971		
		4x 155mm	4x 155mm	4x 155mm	4x 105mm	3x 130mm		
Art.Gr. Hammerfest	II./HKAA.971	HKB 3/971	HKB 16/971	HKB 17/971	HKB 18/971	HKB 19/971	MKB 1/514	MKB 5/514
		4x 105mm	6x 155mm	4x 155mm	4x 105mm	4x 105mm	3x 130mm	4x 100mm
Art.Gr. Nordkapp	IV./HKAA.971	HKB 1/971	HKB 2/971	HKB 8/971	MKB 2/514			
		6x 145mm	4x 105mm	4x 105mm	4 x 170mm			
Art.Gr. Alta	MAA.514	HKB 36/971	HKB 37/971	MKB 3/514	MKB 4/514	MKB 6/514	MKB 7/514	
		4x 155mm	4x 155mm	4x 155mm	3x 130mm	4x 150mm	4x 105mm	
Art.Gr. Oksfjord	III./HKAA.971	HKB 32/971	HKB 33/971	HKB 34/971				
		4x 155mm	4x 155mm	6x 155mm				
Art.Gr. Nordreisa	I./HKAA.972	HKB 33/971	HKB 2/972	HKB 3/972				
		6x 145mm	4x 105mm	4x 105mm				
Art.Gr. Varto	MAA.448	HKB 4/971	HKB 31/971	HKB 1/972	HKB 4/972	HKB 5/972		
		4x 155mm	4x 155mm	6x 145mm	4x 155mm	4x 105mm		

Art.Gr. Ullsfjord	MAA.512	HKB 3/480	HKB 5/480	HKB 8/971	HKB 35/971	HKB 6/972	HKB 7/972	MKB 5/512
		4x 145mm	4x 145mm	4x 105mm	4x 155mm	6x 145mm	4x 105mm	4x 150mm
Art.Gr. Tromso	HKAA.773	HKB 18/971	HKB 8/972	MKB 2/512				
		4x 105mm	4x 105mm	4x 105mm				
Art.Gr. Balsfjord	IV./HKAA.971	HKB 37/971	HKB 16/972	HKB 17/972	HKB 18/972	HKB 999	MKB 1/512	
		4x 155mm	4x 105mm	3x 210mm	3x 210mm	4x 120mm	4x 105mm	
Art.Gr. Senja	II./HKAA.972	HKB 2/480	HKB 19/972	HKB 20/972	HKB 21/972	HKB 22/972	MKB 4/512	
		4x 105mm	4x 105mm	4x 105mm	4x 105mm	4x 155mm	3x 150mm	
Art.Gr. Gavlfjord	HKAA.480	HKB 1/480	HKB 4/448	HKB 34/971				
		4x 105mm	4x 155mm	6x 155mm				
Art.Gr. Vagsfjord	MAA.511	MKB 1/511	MKB 2/511	MKB 3/511	MKB 5/511	MKB 6/511	MKB 7/511	
		3x 170mm	3x 105mm	4x 155mm	4x 406mm	4x 150mm	3x 210mm	
Art.Gr. Harstad	II./HKAA.971	HKB 5/983	HKB 6/983					
		4x 155mm	4x 155mm					
Art.Gr. Andfjord	II./HKAA.983	HKB 12/983	HKB 13/983	HKB 14/983	HKB 15/983			
		4x 155mm	4x 155mm	4x 145mm	6x 155mm			
Art.Gr. Salangen	I./HKAA.983	HKB 1/983	HKB 2/983	HKB 3/983				
		4x 155mm	6x 150mm	3x 210mm				
Art.Gr. Narvik	III./HKAA.973	HKB 31/973	HKB 32/973	HKB 33/973	HKB 34/973	HKB 35/973	HKB 36/973	HKB 37/973
		3x 210mm	3x 210mm	4x 105mm	6x 155mm	4x 105mm	4x 120mm	4x 105mm
Art.Ob.Gr. Vest-Lofoten	HKAA.971							
Art.Gr. Hadsel	I./HKAA.971	HKB 16/971	HKB 46/973	HKB 49/973				
		6x 155mm	6x 155mm	4x 105mm				
Art.Gr. Flakstad	III./HKAA.971	HKB 5/448	HKB 4/480	HKB 2/971	HKB 5/971	HKB 32/971	HKB 36/971	
		3x 210mm	6x 155mm	4x 105mm	4x 155mm	4x 155mm	4x 155mm	
Art.Gr. Moskenes	5./MAA.514	MKB 2/514	MKB 5/514					
		4x 170mm	6x 155mm					
Art.Gr. Vestvagoy	MAA.514	MKB 1/514	MKB 4/514	MKB 6/514	HKB 3/971			
		3x 130mm	3x 130mm	3x 130mm	4x 105mm			
Art.Gr. Svolvær	IV./HKAA.973	HKB 47/973	HKB 48/973					
		6x 155mm	4x 105mm					
Art.Ob.Gr. Lodingen	MAR.30							
Art. Gr. Ofotfjord	3./ MAA 516	MKB 2/516	MKB 3/516					
		4x 150mm	4x 305mm					
Art.Gr. Korsnes	V./HKAA.973	HKB 61/973	HKB 62/973	HKB 63/973	HKB 64/973			
		4x 105mm	4x 105mm	4x 105mm	4x 105mm			
Art.Gr. Vestfjord	MAA.516	MKB 1/516	MKB 4/516	MKB 5/516	MKB 7/516	MKB 8/516		
		4x 150mm	3x 406mm	4x 150mm	4x 100mm	4x 105mm		

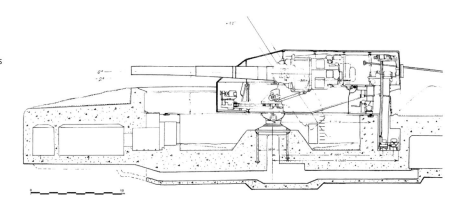

The most powerful of the coastal guns deployed in Norway was Batterie Trondenes I armed with a 406mm SKL/45 "Adolfkanone." This scale plan from a US Army report shows its pedestal mounting in a lightly armored turret. (NARA)

about 2,200 guns deployed on the *Atlantikwall* in France. The three most numerous types in Norway were French, the Schneider 105mm mle 1913 (K331(f): 231 guns, 58 batteries); Schneider 105mm mle. 1936 (K332(f): 95 guns, 24 batteries) and the Schneider 155mm mle 1917 (K416(f): 109 guns, 21 batteries). The most widely used German gun was the obsolete 21cm Mörser 18 with 40 in service in Norway in 13 batteries. Deployment by caliber was as described in Table 5.

By 1944, the Wehrmacht in Norway eventually deployed a total of 12 naval coastal artillery battalions and 11 army coast artillery battalions. Both types of artillery formations were under naval command, subordinate to a special artillery staff at the regional Seeko headquarters. Due to the distances involved, as well as the confusing geographic intermixture of naval and army batteries, the Wehrmacht in Norway decided to create an intermediate artillery command structure not usually found elsewhere on the *Atlantikwall*, the Artillery Group (Art. Gp.: *Artilleriegruppe*), which controlled mixed naval and army batteries as detailed below. Some of these groups were fairly large, with several gun batteries as well as associated torpedo and radar batteries. As a result, some of the larger artillery groups were in turn broken down into tactical artillery sub-groups (*Artillerie-Untergruppe*) to control a specific objective, such as a fjord. In the cases of Bergen and Narvik, the sheer number of batteries in these sectors forced the creation of three super groups to coordinate the artillery formations. Art.Ob.Gr. (*Artillerie-Obergruppen*) Førde controlled the artillery groups in the Bergen area, Art.Ob.Gr. Vest-Lofoten controlled five artillery groups on the southern approaches to Narvik, and Art.Ob.Gr. Lødingen controlled three artillery groups in the Harstad area on the northern Narvik approaches. In contrast to other areas of the *Atlantikwall* such as France and the Netherlands, there were few dedicated flak regiments for coastal defense. Instead, flak batteries were deployed within the army coastal artillery regiments.

A view during the construction of Batterie Trondenes I of MKB 5/511 near Harstad shortly before its completion in the summer of 1943 gives some idea of the size of the weapon. (NARA)

Table 7: coastal batteries, Admiral North Coast

Artillery group	Command unit						
Art.Gr. Folda	I./HKAA.974	HKB 1/971	HKB 7/971	HKB 1/974	HKB 2/974	HKB 3/974	HKB 8/974
		6x 145mm	4x 105mm	6x 155mm	4x 105mm	6x 210mm	4x 88mm
Art.Gr. Bodo	MAA.510	HKB 4/974	HKB 5/974	HKB 6/974	HKB 7/974	HKB 9/974	HKB 10/974	MKB 4/510
		3x 210mm	4x 105mm	6x 155mm	4x 105mm	5x 155mm	4x 105mm	4x 150mm
		MKB 5/510	MKB 6/510				
		4x 150mm	4x 150mm				
Art.Gr. Sandessjoen	II./HKAA.974	HKB 16/974	HKB 17/974	HKB 18/974	HKB 19/974	HKB 20/974	HKB 21/974	HKB 22/974
		4x 155mm	4x 75mm	4x 105mm	4x 105mm	4x 155mm	4x 105mm	4x105mm
		MKB 1/510	MKB 2/510	MKB 3/510			
		4x 127mm	4x 120mm	4x 105mm			
Art.Gr. Bronnoysund	III.HKAA.974	HKB 31/974	HKB 32/974	HKB 33/974			
		6x 155mm	4x 155mm	4x 105mm			
Art.Gr. Vikna	MAA.500	HKB 1/975	MKB 1/500	MKB 2/500			
		4x 75mm	4x 127mm	4x 127mm			
Art.Gr. Namsos	I./HKAA.975	HKB 2/975	HKB 3/975	HKB 4/975	HKB 5/975	HKB 6/975	HKB 7/975	HKB 8/975
		6x 155mm	4x 105mm	4x 105mm	4x 105mm	3x 210mm	5x 155mm	5x 105mm
Art.Gr. Orlandet	MAA.507	HKB 16/975	HKB 18/975	HKB 19/975	MKB 1/507	MKB 4/507	
		5x 105mm	4x 105mm	6x 150mm	3x 280mm	3x 280mm	
Art.Gr. Trondheim-Ost	MAA.506	MKB 1/506	MKB 2/506	MKB 3/506	MKB 4/506	MKB 5/506	HKB 17/975
		3x 150mm+ 2x 210mm	4x 150mm+ 2x 210mm	4x 150mm	3x 120mm	3x 105mm	3x 150mm
Art.Gr. Trondheim-Vest	II./HKAA.975	HKB 20/975	HKB 21/975	HKB 22/975	HKB 23/975	HKB 24/975	HKB 25/975	HKB 26/975
		4x 155mm	6x 210mm	4x 150mm	4x 155mm	4x 76mm	4x 76mm	4x 76mm
		HKB 27/975	HKB 6/971	HKB 2/976			
		4x 105mm	4x 155mm	4x 105mm			
Art.Gr. Kristiansund	I./HKAA.976	HKB 3/976	HKB 4/976	HKB 5/976	HKB 6/976	HKB 7/976	MKB 3/505
		4x 120mm	4x 88mm	4x 105mm	4x 105mm	4x 155mm	3x 150mm
Art.Gr. More	MAA.505	HKB 16/976	HKB 17/976	HKB 18/976	HKB 24/976	HKB 25/976	MKB 1/505
		4x 88mm	6x 155mm	6x 155mm	4x 105mm	4x 88mm	4x 105mm
Art.Gr. Romsdal	II./HKAA.976	HKB 19/976	HKB 20/976	HKB 21/976	HKB 22/976		
		4x 105mm	3x 210mm	6x 155mm	4x 105mm		
Art.Gr. Alesund	III.HKAA.976	HKB 23/976	HKB 30/976	HKB 31/976	HKB 32/976	HKB 33/976	HKB 34/976	MKB 2/505
		4x 105mm	4x 88mm	4x 105mm	4x 105mm	4x 105mm	4x 88mm	3x 150mm
Art.Gr. Stadlandet	IV./HKAA.976	HKB 35/976	HKB 36/976	HKB 37/976	HKB 38/976		
		4x 105mm	4x 105mm	4x 105mm	6x 155mm		

Table 8: coastal batteries, Admiral West Coast

Artillery group	Command unit							
Art. Ob. Gr. Forde	HKAA.981	HKB 5/981						
Art.Gr. Nordfjord	I./HKAA.981	HKB 1/981	HKB 2/981	HKB 3/981	HKB 4/981	HKB 6/981	HKB 17/981	MKB 9/504
		4x 155mm	4x 105mm	4x 105mm	4x 105mm	4x 105mm	4x 105mm	3x 130mm
Art.Gr. Sognefjord	HKAA.981	HKB 11/981	HKB 12/981	HKB 13/981	HKB 14/981	HKB 15/981	HKB 16/981	MKB 7/504
		4x 105mm	4x 88mm	4x 105mm	4x 100mm	4x 100mm	4x 105mm	4x 127mm
Art.Gr. Hjeltefjord	III./HKAA.977	HKB 31/977	HKB 32/977	HKB 33/977	HKB 34/977	HKB 35, 37/977	HKB 38/977	MKB 5/504
		4x 145mm	5x 155mm	4x210mm	4x 105mm	4+ 4x 88mm	5x 105mm	3x 150mm
Art.Gr. Bergen	MAA.504	HKB 36/977	MKB 1/504	MKB 2/504	MKB 3/504	MKB 4/504	MKB 11/504	
		4x 105mm	3x 210mm	3x 240mm	3x 240mm	3x 210mm	3x 280mm	
Art.Gr. Korsfjord	IV./HKAA.977	HKB 46/977	HKB 47/977	HKB 48/977	HKB 49/977	HKB 50/977	MKB 6/504	MKB 8/504
		4x 88mm	3x 210mm	4x 100mm	4x 105mm	4x 100mm	4x 150mm	4x 127mm
Art.Gr. Bomlafjord	IV./HKAA.977	HKB 61/977	HKB 62/977	HKB 63/977				
		4x 88mm	4x 88mm	6x 155mm				
Art.Gr. Haugesund	V./HKAA.977	HKB 64/977	HKB 65/977	HKB 66/977	HKB 68/977	MKB 10/504		
		3x 210mm	4x 145mm	6x 155mm	4x 75mm	4x 150mm		
Art.Gr. Karmoy-Syd	IV./HKAA.978	HKB 1/978	HKB 2/978	HKB 3/978	HKB 67/977			
		6x 155mm	4x 105mm	4x 122mm	4x 145mm			
Art.Gr. Stavanger-Havn	6./HKAA.978	HKB 4/978	HKB 6/978	MKB 1/503				
		4x 150mm	4x 100mm	3x 100mm				
Art.Gr. Stavanger-Syd	I./HKAA.978	HKB 8/978	HKB 9/978	HKB 16/978	HKB 17/978	MKB 3/503	MKB 6/503	
		4x 100mm	4x 210mm	4x 100mm	4x 105mm	4x 170mm	4x 240mm	
Art.Gr. Egersund	II./HKAA.978	HKB 18/978	HKB 19/978	HKB 20/978	MKB 4/503			
		4x 88mm	4x 210mm	4x 100mm	4x 127mm			
Art.Gr. Vanse	III./HKAA.978	HKB 21/978	HKB 22/978	HKB 23/978	HKB 24/978	HKB 25/978	MKB 5/503	
		4x 105mm	4x 105mm	6x 150mm	4x 105mm	4x 105mm	3x 150mm	
Art.Gr. Mandal/Sogne	II./HKAA.979	HKB 17/979	HKB 18/979	HKB 19/979	HKB 20/979	HKB 21/979		
		4x 105mm	4x 105mm	4x 155mm	4x 105mm	4x 105mm		
Art.Gr. Kristiansand	MAA.502	MKB 1/502	MKB 2/502	MKB 3/502	MKB 5/502	MKB 6/502		
		3x 150mm	3x 150mm	2x 210mm	4x 240mm	3x 380mm		
Art.Gr. Lillesand	III./HKAA.979	HKB 31/979	HKB 32/979					
		4x 105mm	4x 105mm					
Art.Gr. Arendal	III./HKAA.979	HKB 33/979	HKB 34/979	HKB 35/979	HKB 36/979	HKB 37/979		
		4x 105mm	4x 105mm	4x 105mm	4x 105mm	4x 105mm		
Art.Gr. Larvik	I./HKAA.980	HKB 1/980	HKB 2/980	HKB 3/980	HKB 4/980	HKB 5/980		
		4x 105mm	4x 105mm	4x 120mm	4x 88mm	4x 120mm		

Art.Gr. Makeroy	MAA.501	HKB 8/980	MKB 3/501	MKB 4/501	MKB 6/501	MKB 5/501	MKB 2/501	
		4x 105mm	4x 150mm	4x 150mm	3x 380mm	3x 280mm	4x 150mm	
Art.Gr. Fredrikstad	II./HKAA.980	HKB 6/980	HKB 7/980	HKB 17/971				
		4x 100mm	4x 100mm	4x 155mm				

Note:

Coastal artillery units in Norway were designated in an alternate format than elsewhere on the Atlantikwall. The format for batteries in Norway was, for example, HKB 6/908 where HKB or MKB identifies army or navy battery, prefix (6) identifies battery number, suffix (908) identifies parent regiment. The standard format for battalions elsewhere was, for example, 1./HKAA.980 where numeral prefix (1.) identifies the battery, a Roman numeral prefix (II.) identifies a battalion, and a numerical suffix (980) identifies parent regiment.

By far the most spectacular coastal artillery in Norway were the three dozen heavy naval guns, usually surplus warship weapons, assigned to critical defensive assignments. The most powerful of these weapons were the "Adolfkanonen," a set of 406mm guns originally intended for the never-completed H-class battleships. They were installed in the islands shielding Narvik and were intended to cover all sea approaches to this port. The Vara battery near Kristiansand on

Although gun casemates were relatively uncommon in Norway compared with other sections of the *Atlantikwall*, some of the more important batteries in the south were reinforced. Batterie Vara of MKB 6/502 covering the Skaggerak with its three 380mm SKC/34 guns was scheduled to be moved to this impressive S169 casemate, but it was never completed. It is seen here during an inspection of US Army officers immediately after the war. (NARA)

Table 9: heavy coastal guns in Norway					
Battery	**Unit**	**Location**	**Number**	**Type**	**Source**
Batterie Trondenes I	MKB 5/511	Harstad	4	405mm SKC/34	H-class battleship project
Batterie Engelöy	MKB 4/516	Engelöy island	3	405mm SKC/34	H-class battleship project
Batterie Vara	MKB 6/502	Movik	3	38cm SKC/34	battlecruiser projects
Batterie Nötteröy	MKB 6/501	Vardasen	3	38cm KM36/35(f)	French battleship *Jean-Bart*
Batterie Lödingen	MKB 3/516	Makeroy	4	305mm Bofors L/30	pre-war Norwegian coastal gun
Batterie Husoen	MKB 1/507	Ostersjoomradet	3	28cm SKL/45	cruiser *Goeben*
Batterie Kiberg	MKB 3/513	Husaen	3	28cm SKL/45	WWI warships
Batterie Örlandet	MKB 4/507	Örlandet	3	28cm SKC/34 (triple)	battleship *Gneisenau*
Batterie Fjell	MKB 11/504	Fjell	3	28cm SKC/34 (triple)	battleship *Gneisenau*
Batterie Mestersand	MKB 4/517	Sylt	4	24cm SKL/40	pre-1900 battleships and cruisers

Table 10: Kriegsmarine torpedo batteries in Norway

Battery	Torpedo	Artillery Group	Local naval command
Torpedobatterie Bokfjord	4x 53cm	Art. Gr. Un. Sydvaranger	MAA.513
Torpedobatterie Porsoy	2x 53cm	Art. Gr. Ofotfjord	MAA.516
Torpedobatterie Korshamn	2x 53cm	Art. Gr. Ofotfjord	MAA.516
Torpedobatterie Ledangsholm	4x 53cm	Art. Gr. Namsos	MAA.506
Torpedobatterie Hasselvik (Hysness)	4x 53cm	Art. Gr. Trondheim-ost	MAA.506
Torpedobatterie Hambaara	4x 53cm	Art. Gr. Trondheim-ost	MAA.506
Torpedobatterie Nordlandet	4x 53cm	Art. Gr. More	MAA.505
Torpedobatterie Julholmen	2x 52cm	Art. Gr. More	MAA.505
Torpedobatterie Otteroy syd	2x 52cm	Art. Gr. More	MAA.505
Torpedobatterie Angelshaug (Vemelsvik)	2x 45cm	Art. Gr. Nordfjord	MAA.504
Torpedobatterie Rutledal	2x 45cm	Art. Gr. Sognefjord	MAA.504
Torpedobatterie Hjelte (Herdla)	3x 53cm	Art. Gr. Hjeltefjord	MAA.504
Torpedobatterie Gavlen	2x 45cm	Art. Gr. Hjeltefjord	MAA.504
Torpedobatterie Kvarven	3x 45cm	Art. Gr. Bergen	MAA.504
Torpedobatterie Radne (Leroy)	3x 53cm	Art. Gr. Bergen	MAA.504
Torpedobatterie Ljones	2x 45cm	Art. Gr. Korsfjord	MAA.504
Torpedobatterie Kaholm	3x 45cm	Art. Gr. Makeroy	MAA.501

the Skagerrak was mounted in similar single-gun turrets in an S169 kettle position; a set of massive casemates was under construction but not occupied at the end of the war. Although of less impressive size, many other surplus warship turrets were deployed in Norway including eight 150mm SKC/28 guns in twin C/36 turrets intended for the incomplete *Graf Zeppelin* aircraft carrier.

F BATTERIE TRONDENES I, 5./MAA.511, HARSTAD, NORWAY

The most powerful guns emplaced in Norway were the massive Krupp 406mm Adolfkanonen in two batteries at Steigen and Trondenes, which had a maximum range of 56km (35 miles). The guns were leftovers from the abortive H-class battleships. Since the naval turrets were never completed, the guns were mounted in a special BSG (*Bettungshiess-Gerüst*) single mounting with a turret of light 45mm armor steel. The guns were fitted to an S384 complex, which consisted of a deep concrete well with a high gun pedestal, along with a series of tunnels leading back into reinforced concrete ammunition galleries behind the gun. In contrast to the sister battery in France, Batterie Lindemann near Calais, an overhead casemate was never built for the Norwegian batteries. The turret was covered with a camouflage umbrella constructed of wood outriggers with wire netting garnished with pieces of white and green waxed paper and bunches of dried grass.

Each battery consisted of four gun positions, located about 250m apart. Battery Trondenes I, also known as Batterie Theo, was located on a rocky headland north of Harstad, and positioned to cover the Andfjorden and Vagsfjorden on the northern approaches to Narvik. Its sister, Batterie Dietl, was located on Engeloy to cover the Vestfjorden on the southern approach to Narvik. The four gun positions were located 85–105m above sea level. Construction of the battery started in 1942, but the battery was not entirely complete at war's end. A reserve ammunition bunker and an emergency headquarters for the regional Seeko were still under construction. The battery was protected by an 88mm flak battery and three more light flak batteries (37mm and 77mm) in the area. Batterie Harstad Nord (1./MAA.511) with three 170mm guns was positioned downhill from Batterie Trondenes at the tip of the headlands for sea-level defense.

Batterie Flakfort of 1./MAA.508 covering the Copenhagen roadstead was a former Danish battery equipped with six of these turreted 210mm SKL/51 guns. (NARA)

Table 11: K-Verbände in Norway, 1945		
Unit	**Base**	**Weapons**
1.K-Division	**Narvik**	
K-Flotilla 2/265	Engeloy	11 Biber
K-Flotilla 1/215	Ullvik	30 Linse
K-Flotilla 1/362	Brenvik	20 Marder
MEK.35	Harstad	60 troops
MEK.90	Oslo	30 troops
2.K-Division	**Trondheim**	
K-Flotilla 2/216	Namsos	24 Linse
K-Flotilla 1/216	Selvenas	36 Linse
K-Flotilla 1/267	Kristiansund	15 Biber
K-Flotilla 2/267	Molde	15 Biber
MEK.30	Molde	80 troops
3.K-Division	**Bergen**	
K-Flotilla 1/362	Herdla	20 Marder
K-Flotilla 215	Flatoy	30 Linse
K-Flotilla 2/362	Krokeidet	20 Marder
K-Flotilla 415	Stavanger	30 Molch
K-Flotilla 1/263	Sogne-Hollen	14 Biber
K-Flotilla 2/263	Tangen-Stolsviken	15 Biber
MEK.25	Stend-Bergen	60 troops
4.K-Division	**Oslofjord**	
K-Flotilla 265	Haao	20 Biber
K-Flotilla 1/366	Stavern	15 Marder
K-Flotilla 2/366	Mageroy	15 Marder

Torpedo batteries

The value of torpedo batteries in the defense of Norway's numerous fjords was made painfully apparent to the Kriegsmarine on April 9, 1940 when the cruiser *Blücher* was sunk by two 28cm torpedoes from the Oscarborg fort in Oslofjord. The Norwegian navy had begun establishing torpedo batteries as early as 1890, mounted in concealed underwater launchers. These batteries were positioned to cover passageways that were 5,000m wide or less. Besides taking over several Norwegian batteries and using Norwegian navy equipment to create others, the Kriegsmarine installed their own batteries, eventually totaling 17 shore batteries. In contrast to the original Norwegian batteries, the German batteries typically used destroyer-type triple launch tubes mounted on the surface in a concrete building with a fire-control post located nearby, often supported by a searchlight. A typical battery consisted of three officers and 40 men, and was subordinated to the coastal artillery battalion in the area. In addition to the shore batteries, two floating batteries were deployed in Bergen.

Denmark

Denmark was the most obscure portion of the *Atlantikwall*. Denmark had very modest coastal defenses prior to the 1940 invasion, mainly centered around Copenhagen's harbor. As a short-term expedient, in the summer of 1940 the Wehrmacht deployed 15 navy coastal batteries at the major harbors and major chokepoints leading into the Baltic, based primarily on old war-booty artillery taken from the Danish arsenal. The naval command in Denmark was designated Admiral Skaggerak and was subordinate to the Navy Baltic High Command (*Marine Oberkommando Ostsee*); there were three subordinate Seeko. The Army High Command Denmark (AOK-Dänemark) was the corresponding army command.

The autumn of 1940 saw the first major construction effort with a scheme to deploy two heavy coastal batteries in Denmark: one at Hanstholm opposite Norway to control the Skaggerak, and a pair on Bornholm in the Baltic to cover the Kattegat. In the event, the invasion of the Soviet Union in 1941 curtailed the Bornholm plans, but the Hanstholm project continued along with a corresponding battery on the Norwegian side of the

Skaggerak, Batterie Vara. The Royal Navy raids on the Norwegian coast in early 1941 forced the Wehrmacht to recognize the weak protection on the Danish coast, and in late April 1940 the army decided to deploy ten coastal artillery batteries to Denmark while the navy expanded its coverage, especially the approaches to the Sound and the Small and Great Belts. As in Norway, most of the attention through 1944 was in providing defense for major ports, though in Denmark this effort extended to covering the various chokepoints into the Baltic. Since Denmark was often overflown by Allied bombers on their way to German ports, Denmark had a very substantial Luftwaffe fortification and construction effort with numerous radar and flak sites.

By the summer of 1943, with the *Atlantikwall* program in full bloom in France and the Low Countries, the Wehrmacht began to examine a possible threat of an Allied amphibious landing in western Denmark aimed at reaching northern Germany. The most likely landing areas were considered to be northern Jutland or the Esbjerg area. One of the immediate outcomes of this assessment was to substantially augment the coastal batteries on Fano Island off Esbjerg as well as gun batteries to defend the port itself; 12 more army artillery batteries were also allotted to Denmark. Four areas were declared Defense Zones (*Verteidigungsbereiche*): Esbjerg, Hansted, Frederikshavn and Aalborg. The various infantry and artillery positions were consolidated into strongpoint groups for greater unity of command and a total of 20 of these groups were organized, seven of which were airbases rather than coastal defense sectors.

In spite of the Normandy invasion in June 1944, the Wehrmacht continued to be concerned over threats to Denmark, based on the mistaken intelligence assessment that the Allies were withholding forces for possible operations against Denmark or Norway. The Kriegsmarine was convinced that the greatest threat was against the Kattegat on the eastern Jutland coast, the presumption being that Allied actions to control this area would block U-boats constructed in the Baltic ports from reaching their new operating bases in Norway. As a result, a program to add 29 naval batteries was begun. In contrast, Hitler and the army were more concerned about the threat posed to the western coast of Jutland as a potential shortcut into northern Germany. This resulted in the construction of three inland blocking positions, codenamed the Brunhild, Gudrun and Kriehild lines, consisting of antitank ditches and field fortifications rather than elaborate concrete fortifications. By late 1944, the situation was even more

ABOVE LEFT
This is one of the turreted St. Chamond 210mm guns of MKB 3/502 at Flekkeroy first deployed in the summer of 1940. Like many of the heavy gun positions in Norway, the lack of overhead casemate protection led to more extensive efforts at camouflage, sometimes including elaborate metal frames for its camouflage umbrella. (NARA)

ABOVE RIGHT
Verteidigungsbereich Hansted was the most heavily defended sector on the Danish coast, covering the southern shores of the Skaggerak opposite Kristiansand in Norway. The first major fortified battery constructed there was Hanstholm I, begun in May 1940, armed with these old 1902 German 170mm naval guns. These were deployed in M270 casemates and the battery was manned by 1./MAA.118. (NARA)

BELOW
Coastal torpedo batteries were most common in Norway due to their value in covering narrow fjords. This is one of the two 53cm launchers of Torpedobatterie Korshamn of MAA.516 at Ofotfjorden. (NARA)

TOP LEFT

The cruiser *Gneisenau* served as the source for several heavy batteries in the Netherlands and Scandinavia, including Batterie Stordal of 2./MAA.518 on Fano Island in Denmark that was constructed late in 1944, armed with a twin 150mm SK L/55 in a C/28 turret on an M 184 bunker. This battery was preserved after the war. (NARA)

TOP RIGHT

One of the more common turreted guns found in the Netherlands and Denmark was the dual-purpose 105mm SK C/32 naval anti-aircraft gun seen here as part of the VB Hansted defenses, manned by MFA.814. The armored turret is completely covered in camouflage net with paper or metal garnishing. (NARA)

Table 12: Kriegsmarine Coastal Artillery Batteries in Denmark

MAA.134	Sylt	8./MAA.134				
		4 x 76mm				
MAA.518	Esbjerg	2./MAA.518	3./MAA.518	4./MAA.518		
		4x 150mm	4x 150mm	4x 380mm		
MAA.118	Hanstholm	1./MAA.118	2./MAA.118	3./MAA.118		
		4x 170mm	4x 380mm	4x 120mm		
MAA.509	Lokken	1./MAA.509	2./MAA.509	3./MAA.509	4./MAA.509	5./MAA.509
		4x 105mm	4x 120mm	8x 120mm	4x 127mm	4x 150mm
MAA.521	Hals	1./MAA.521	2./MAA.521	3./MAA.521	4./MAA.521	5./MAA.521
		4x 150mm	4x 88mm	4x 88mm	4x 127mm	4x 75mm
		6./MAA.521	7./MAA.521			
		4x 75mm	4x 305mm			
MAA.523	Grena	2./MAA.523	3./MAA.523	4./MAA.523	5./MAA.523	6./MAA.523
		4x 75mm	4x 75mm	4x 75mm	4x 105mm	4x 75mm
MAA.524	Arhus	2./MAA.524	3./MAA.524	4./MAA.524	5./MAA.524	6./MAA.524
		4x 105mm	4x 105mm	4x 75mm	4x 75mm	3x 105mm
MAA.522	Nykobing	3./MAA.522	4./MAA.522	5./MAA.522	6./MAA.522	7./MAA.522
		4x 75mm	4x 150mm	4x 75mm	4x 75mm	4x 127mm
		8./MAA.522	10./MAA.522	11./MAA.522	12./MAA.522	
		4x 75mm	4x 105mm	3x 88mm	4x 75mm	
MAA.508	Copenhagen	1./MAA.508	2./MAA.508	3./MAA.508	4./MAA.508	5./MAA.508
		6x 210mm	4x 120mm	4x 88mm	4x 75mm	4x 150mm
		6./MAA.508	7./MAA.508	8./MAA.508		
		4x 75mm	12x 170mm+ 6x 305mm	4x 127mm		

Table 13: Kriegsmarine Coastal Flak Batteries in Denmark

MFA.234	Sylt	7./MFA.234			
		4x 75mm			
MFA.204	Esbjerg	2./MFA.204	3./MFA.204	4./MFA.204	5./MFA.204
		4x 105mm	4x 105mm	4x 105mm	4x 105mm
MFA.814	Hanstholm	2./MFA.814	3./MFA.814	4./MFA.814	5./MFA.814
		4x 105mm	4x 105mm	4x 105mm	4x 105mm
MFA.716	Frederikshavn	2./MFA.716	3./MFA.716	4./MFA.716	
		4x 105mm	4x 105mm	4x 75mm	
MFA.717	Arhus	2./MFA.717	3./MFA.717	4./MFA.717	5./MFA.717
		4x 88mm	4x 75mm	4x 88mm	4x 75mm

Table 14: Army Coastal Artillery Batteries in Denmark

I./HKAR.180	Vemb	II./HKAR.180	Vrögum	III./HKAR.180	Hjörring
1./HKAR.180	4x 105mm	6./HKAR.180	4x 105mm	9./HKAR.180	4x 105mm
2./HKAR.180	4x 105mm	7./HKAR.180	4x 105mm	10./HKAR.180	4x 105mm
3./HKAR.180	4x 105mm	8./HKAR.180	4x 105mm	20./HKAR.180	4x 122mm
4./HKAR.180	4x 105mm	11./HKAR.180	4x 122mm	21./HKAR.180	4x 122mm
5./HKAR.180	4x 105mm	12./HKAR.180	4x 122mm		
17./HKAR.180	4x 194mm	13./HKAR.180	4x 122mm		
18./HKAR.180	4x 122mm	14./HKAR.180	4x 150mm		
19./HKAR.180	4x 122mm	15./HKAR.180	4x 122mm		
20./HKAR.180	6x 152mm	16./HKAR.180	4x 122mm		

unsettled due to the advance of the Red Army from the east as well as Soviet naval operations in the Baltic. In consequence, AOK-Dänemark was overruled, and priority for defensive construction shifted to the Kattegat coastline, as recommended by the navy. The Kriegsmarine planned to deploy 20 more batteries in early 1945, but the collapse of the German war economy prevented this; in April 1945 there were substantial shifts of coastal gun batteries from Denmark to the Eastern front. Likewise, there was considerable turmoil in the army coastal artillery batteries as AOK-Dänemark realized that the more likely threat to Denmark was not an Allied amphibious invasion, but an Allied advance into Denmark from the south via Germany. A number of the army coastal batteries were moved to the southern portion of Denmark to set up a new defense line. In total, 22 army and 46 navy coastal artillery batteries were deployed in Denmark during the war, though the number was in flux through most of 1944–45. The navy also deployed 16 flak batteries for the defense of major ports.

THE SITES IN COMBAT

Of the four countries surveyed in this book, only the Netherlands endured significant combat along its stretch of the *Atlantikwall*. Belgium's short coast was liberated by the Canadian Army during the lightning advance of September 1944. Norway experienced some limited fighting in October 1944 when the Red Army stormed the arctic Finnmark region, chasing the Wehrmacht out of Finland. However, this did not involve extensive combat along the *Atlantikwall*. Denmark experienced no significant combat on its portion of the *Atlantikwall*.

The Scheldt campaign

Although the British Army captured Antwerp in mid-September 1944, the opportunity to bounce the Rhine by airborne assault with Operation *Market-Garden* distracted Allied attention from the pressing need to clear both banks of the Scheldt Estuary. Without control of the Scheldt the port of Antwerp was useless, since maritime traffic could be interdicted by the numerous German coastal batteries on either side. Without the supplies that could have been delivered through Antwerp, the Allied advance stalled in the autumn of 1944. Following the defeat at Arnhem, Eisenhower insisted that Montgomery's 21st Army Group refocus its attention on the Scheldt mission.

By the third week of September, the Wehrmacht also had realized the critical importance of the Scheldt and began a deliberate effort to reinforce the positions on both banks of the river. Hitler designated the Breskens pocket on the south bank as *Festung Schelde Sud* while the island of Walcheren and South Beveland to the north was designated as *Festung Schelde Nord*. This change in designation had little to do with any reinforcement of the fortification, rather it was a symbolic gesture as Hitler had ordered all *Festungen* to be held to the last man. On September 15, the 70.Infanterie Division took over defense of Walcheren and South Beveland while by September 18, the 64.Infanterie Division took up positions in the Breskens pocket. The 64th was a Russian front veteran and by far the more stubborn foe; the 70th was a so-called "stomach" division filled out with troops with medical problems and designated as a static division for coastal defense tasks. The defense of the Breskens pocket was aided considerably by the barriers presented by the Canal-de-la-Lys and the Leopold Canal as well as flooded areas associated with them. There had been some efforts made in 1944 to create a *Landfront* south of Breskens consisting of some pillboxes. Although there were five major coastal artillery batteries in the Breskens pocket, they had a limited role in the subsequent fighting as their casemates kept the guns pointed out to sea. The 3rd Canadian Division secured a penetration over the Leopold Canal on October 6, 1944, and followed this with an amphibious landing from Terneuzen around the eastern shoulder of the Breskens pocket on October 9. In spite of these successes, the 64.Infanterie Division waged a determined defense and the pocket was not cleared until early November.

In the meantime, the 2nd Canadian Division had been assigned to clear South Beveland by pushing up the narrow isthmus from the east. The difficulty of this assault led to a bold decision to lift two battalions from the British 52nd Division across the Scheldt using amphibious Buffalo LVT (landing vehicle, tracked) of the 79th Armoured Division, supported by Sherman DD amphibious tanks on October 26. The 2nd Canadian Division pushed across South Beveland and reached the narrow causeway to Walcheren on October 31.

After the success of the 52nd Division amphibious operation, another more ambitious operation was scheduled for Walcheren. Earlier in the month, RAF Bomber Command had struck at the Westkapelle dike, breaching it and flooding most of the island. This complicated the German defense effort, but about half the German coastal batteries were still high and dry on the dikes. The amphibious assault was a two-pronged operation consisting of Operation *Infatuate I*, another river landing by the 52nd Division against Vlissingen (Flushing) using the amphibious equipment of the 79th Armoured Division; and *Infatuate II* by the 4th Special Service Brigade landing by sea against Westkapelle.

The town of Vlissingen had been heavily fortified as MKB Kernwerk Vlissingen and included 9./MAA.202. The decision to stage the landing in the predawn hours substantially reduced casualties during the landing phase, but the fighting for the town proved more difficult due to the numerous bunkers and pillboxes.

The Westkapelle landing zone was imperiled by the presence of three coastal artillery batteries of MAA.202. MKB Westkapelle of 6./MAA.202, identified as "W15" in British documents, was armed with four British 3.7in. anti-aircraft guns captured at Dunkirk supported by two 75mm guns that were in gun pits. This battery was part of Strongpoint Tiefland defended by 5./Grenadier Regiment 1018. The neighboring MKB Zoutelande of 7./MAA.202 ("W13") was armed with four 150mm TbtK C/36 naval guns in Bauform 671 casemates reinforced by two 75mm guns in Bauform 612 casemates. It was part of Strongpoint Rheingold held by 5./Grenadier Regiment 1018. Besides the coastal batteries in the landing zone, MKB Domburg of 5./MAA.202 ("W17") near Zoutelande had four French 220mm guns in open pits, which were in easy reach of the landing area. Although there had been some RAF strikes against the batteries, the main guns were functional at the time of the British landings.

The British amphibious force heading towards Westkapelle on the morning of November 1 included gun- and rocket-firing support craft as well as the battleship HMS *Warspite* and the monitors *Erebus* and *Roberts*. The gun battle between the Royal Navy and MAA.202 began shortly after 0800 hours with *Warspite* bombarding W17, *Roberts* versus W13 and *Erebus* versus W15. In the event, *Erebus* suffered a failure of its turret traverse, and so *Roberts* was obliged to engage two gun batteries. The Royal Navy Close Support Squadron had its gun and rocket craft split into two groups, planning to distract the German gunners from the vulnerable infantry landing craft. Two LCT(R) rocket craft of the Southern Group were hit by MKB Zoutelande, but managed to retire after firing most of their rockets. The group's nine gun support craft attempted to engage the German bunkers, but most were severely damaged in a very unequal duel with the bunkers. The situation with the Northern Group was not much better, and an accident with one of the rocket craft resulted in several rockets striking two of the gun craft. Once again, the heavily protected MKB Westkapelle had the better of the gun duels, severely damaging most of the gun support craft. Of 27 support craft taking place in the operation, ten were sunk and six were severely damaged; 172 sailors were killed or missing and 125 wounded. The sacrifice of the gun support craft had not been in vain as the 4th Special Service Brigade landed at Westkapelle largely intact starting at 0957. By the time the landing craft went ashore, MKB Zoutelande had run out of ammunition. MKB Westkapelle continued to fire and damaged two

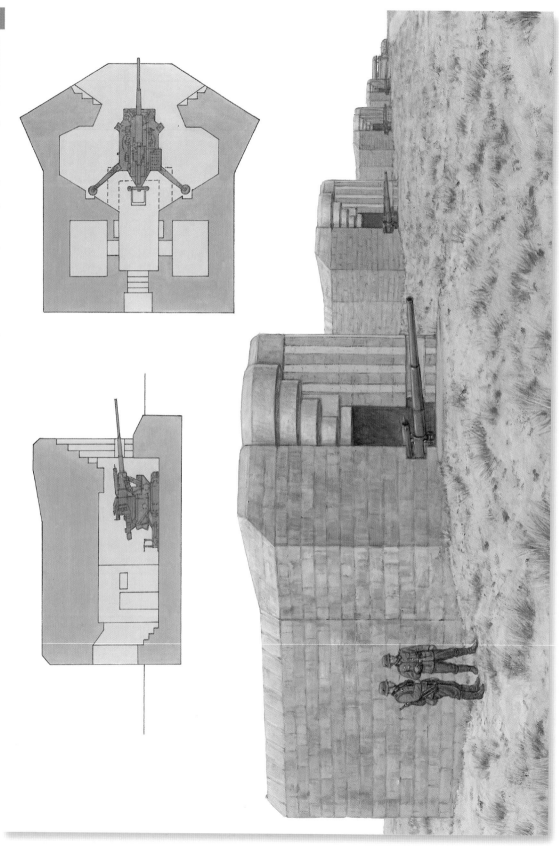

Batterie Westkapelle, 6./MAA.202, Westkapelle, Walcheren, The Netherlands

more tank landing craft; the battery was finally cleared by 41 Royal Marine Commando around noon while MKB Zoutelande was overrun by 48 Royal Marine Commando in the early afternoon. The MKB Domburg position was not taken until the next day. Although MAA.202 had failed to stop the landings, these two units were arguably the most destructive of any *Atlantikwall* gun batteries during the war.

K-Verbände in the Netherlands

The Kriegsmarine recognized the importance of Antwerp and lacking means to interdict the port, assigned the K-Verbände the task of attacking Allied shipping. The operations got off to a poor start on the night of October 5/6 when K-Flotilla.214 supported by the MEK.60 commandos attempted to attack Allied minesweepers from their base in Groningen. The small boats were unseaworthy in typical autumn North Sea conditions, and after losing nearly half their boats the flotilla had to be returned to Germany for rebuilding without accomplishing anything; their place was taken by K-Flotilla.215. Their poor performance on combat missions led to schemes to use the boats to resupply isolated German garrisons at Dunkirk and in the Breskens pocket. These October missions flopped due to the limited capacity of the boats and their vulnerability to sea conditions. The K-Verbände attempted to use them in the calmer waters of the Scheldt, and a raid was conducted on the night of October 23 against Allied ports supporting operations on South Beveland with meager results. The boat flotillas were ineffective and Admiral Heye recommended that they be held in reserve as a potential counterattack force for any Allied amphibious landings in North

TOP LEFT
Kernwerk Vlissingen was heavily fortified along the Scheldt and this is a Bauform 143 artillery observation bunker of WN Leuchtenburg near the Orange Mole on the south side of the port. This bunker has been restored by the Bunkerbehoud foundation and the guardrails are a postwar safety measure. (Author's photograph)

TOP RIGHT
This is one of the Bauform 671 casemates of MKB Westkapelle of 6./MAA.202 (W15) armed with British 3.7-inch anti-aircraft guns during the brutal gun duels fought during the landings on Walcheren in November 1944. Two of the casemates were blown up by British engineers after the battle, and these surviving two were later demolished after the war. This is a Dutch Army photo taken in 1946 after the casemate had been disarmed. (Nederlands Instituut voor Militaire Historie)

G   **BATTERIE WESTKAPELLE, 6./MAA.202, WESTKAPELLE, WALCHEREN, THE NETHERLANDS**

This battery, better known by its British map designation as W15, was one of the two batteries of Kapitan Robert Opalka's MAA.202 which fiercely resisted the British landings on Walcheren on November 1, 1944. This battery consisted of four Bauform 671 SK gun casemates armed with four British 3.7-inch anti-aircraft guns captured at Dunkirk. The battery was supported by an M262 fire control post at the southern end. The Bauform 671 was one of the most common types of *Atlantikwall* casemates with 96 in the Netherlands, 59 in Denmark, 86 in Norway and 254 in France. The embrasure offered 120 degrees of traverse but at the same time, the crew was exposed to hostile fire with no gun shield on these weapons. This casemate type was categorized as "*ohne Nebenräume*", that is without the larger storerooms sometimes found in the larger casemate types. This type had two small ammunition rooms to either side behind the main gun position (shown in the plan view, above right), and access was by way of an armored door at the rear; the battery had an inventory of 2,628 rounds at the end of October 1944 and fired most of them during the course of the battle. The preferred method of construction was the use of wooden shuttering when the concrete was poured over the steel reinforcing rods. However, an alternate method using an outer shell of prefabricated concrete bricks was sometimes used as in this case.

Holland. A raid against Moerdijk blew up some undefended harbor facilities on the night of November 21, while the Linse operating base at Burgsluis was bombed out of existence on December 4. A raid on December 5 was caught in the open by the RAF, and most of the dozen Linse were sunk. An attempted raid on December 12 cost several more Linse and the remainder of the flotilla was packed up and sent back to Germany for overhaul. Additional Linse were sent to the Netherlands in 1945, but these small craft proved more dangerous to their operators than the Allied navies. The Linse operations had proven so costly and futile that the North Sea commander recommended that operations be halted; Admiral Dönitz insisted they continue, as the Kriegsmarine had few other surface warships aside from S-boats to conduct operations in the North Sea. During the course of 1945, the Linse boats conducted a further 171 sorties and lost 54 boats in the process without sinking any Allied vessels.

The dubious value of the Linse explosive boats led to renewed attention to midget submarines, and besides the inactive K-Flotilla.261 stationed at Pooterhaven since September, two more Biber units, K-Flotilla.262 and 266, were deployed at Groningen in December. Initial operations in mid-December were largely unsuccessful due to the susceptibility of the small submarines to the winter weather, and several were lost at sea before ever engaging Allied ships. A mission by K.Flotilla.261 on the night of December 22 was a disaster, when British MTB torpedo boats intercepted the flotilla while the submarines were being towed to sea by R-boats. Four Bibers were immediately lost, and, of the five that escaped, four more were lost during the course of the raid. Another group of ten Bibers assigned to lay mines in the Scheldt that same evening lost two to mines, another was caught on the surface by a Royal Navy motor launch and sunk, and several more were sunk or damaged by British anti-submarine patrols through the course of December 23. The first success of the flotillas occurred at 16:25 on December 23 when a Biber torpedoed the Panamanian freighter *Alan Dale* destined for Antwerp. Biber attacks petered out later in the month due to the weather, and the Royal Navy claimed 27 captured, sunk or probably sunk, and 16 more possibly sunk.

The winter weather limited operations in the new year. When the attacks resumed in earnest in March 1945, Allied anti-submarine forces were very active, claiming 35 midget subs destroyed in March and 19 in April along with 16 possibly sunk in March and 4 in April; actual losses were much higher, and the K-Verbände lost 70 Biber and Molch midget submarines during 102 sorties. The vulnerability of the K-Verbände was nowhere more evident than the night of March 11/12 when a major operation was staged against shipping in the Scheldt without sinking a single ship while losing 13 Biber, 9 Molch and 16 Linse. During the 1945 actions, the midget submarines primarily relied on minelaying and accounted for seven minor Allied vessels totaling less than 500 tons. The Biber was reinforced by the much more capable Seehund, which operated at sea like a conventional submarine; a detailed treatment of the latter remains outside the scope of this book. Overall, the results of the K-Verbände operations were extremely poor in light of the resources allotted to them, especially compared with the S-boats operating out of their hardened harbor bunkers. As mentioned in the Norwegian section, a far more substantial force was deployed in Norway including four of the five K-Verbände divisions, but they never saw combat.

Combat in Norway

Coastal artillery in Norway saw very little combat during the war. One German officer estimated that the batteries in southern Norway fired about 200 rounds during the war, mostly at night against British small craft. The most extensive engagements took place in December 1944 and January 1945 due to Royal Navy destroyer and cruiser actions off Stavanger involving Battery Egersund. In contrast to the coastal artillery, naval and army flak units that were part of the coastal artillery groups were used on a number of occasions against Allied air raids.

When Finland withdrew from the war on September 4, 1944, the terms of the armistice forced the Wehrmacht to withdraw from Finland. With the Red Army occupying the Baltic coast, this meant a fighting evacuation via northern Finland into the Finnmark area of northern Norway. The Wehrmacht had fortified the area around Petsamo and there was some hope that 19.Gebirgs Korps could hold on to the area, as winter came early in the Arctic and there was the conviction that the Red Army would await better weather. Recognizing their vulnerability, on October 3, 1944 Hitler authorized Operation *Nordlicht* (*Northern Light*), a withdrawal out of northern Finland back to the Lyngen Position, a defensive line along the Lyngen Fjord and the northern tip of Sweden. In the event, the Red Army launched an offensive on October 7, 1944 that overwhelmed the German defensive lines in Finland and led to the capture of Petsamo on October 15. Not content to chase the Wehrmacht out of Finland, the third phase of the Soviet offensive aimed at seizing the Norwegian port of Kirkenes, and this area was captured by the end of the month, bringing the offensive to a close. During the fighting, some of the coastal artillery batteries took part in providing fire support for the harried German defenders, firing about 600 rounds. Many of the mobile batteries were withdrawn from the coast to reinforce the Lyngen Line, and those left behind were usually spiked before their capture by Soviet forces.

The Soviet advance forced the Kriegsmarine to move the battleship *Tirpitz* from its remote anchorage in the Altafjord to Tromso for use as a floating coastal battery. This put the damaged ship within range of RAF Lancasters, which struck the warship on November 12, 1944, finally sinking it after 15 previous attacks by RAF and Royal Navy aircraft.

The last battle

One of the strangest battles on the *Atlantikwall* in the Netherlands occurred in April 1945 on the island of Texel. This fighting was an unintended outcome of German policies in 1943–45 to "dilute" German occupation troops along the *Atlantikwall* with Soviet prisoners of war, who volunteered to serve in the Wehrmacht rather than risk death in the ghastly prison camps. In February 1945, Georgischen Bataillon.822, consisting of about 800 Georgian and 400 German troops, was sent to occupy the infantry defenses of Strongpoint Texel. The unit was part of the paper 219.Infanterie Division organized in March 1945 to free up German troops in the Den Helder defense sector. Besides this unit, there were three coastal artillery batteries on the island along with a number of other German defenses, including a radar post. On the night of April 5/6, 1945 the Georgian troops mutinied and killed most of the German troops in their battalion. They did not manage to overcome the naval batteries MKB Eierland and Hors of 2./ and 3./MAA.607 or the army battery 1./HKAA.1230, which were manned by German troops. While the artillery batteries tied down the mutineers, reinforcements arrived from the mainland,

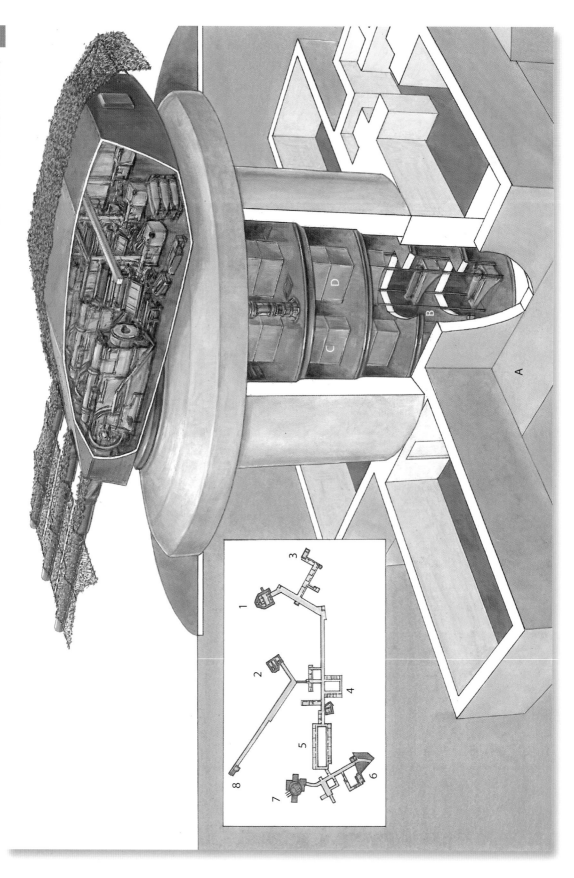

Batterie Fjell, MKB.11/504, Bergen, Norway

mainly Marine-Schützenregiment.163. A violent battle pitting the Georgian troops and Dutch resistance fighters against the Wehrmacht units lasted for two weeks with the Georgians losing about 565 men; about 800 Germans and 117 Dutch civilians also died during the rebellion. The Georgians continued to fight against the Germans even after the May 8 capitulation and Canadian troops did not arrive on the island until May 20, bringing an end to the bloodshed. The lingering fighting on Texel has led this curious encounter to be dubbed "the last battle of World War II."

The K-Verbände midget submarine flotillas in Holland began to receive the improved Molch submarine in 1945. This type carries two torpedoes or mines on the lower hull sides, though this preserved example at the Marshall Museum in Overloon, the Netherlands lacks the weapons. (Author's photograph)

H BATTERIE FJELL, MKB.11/504, BERGEN, NORWAY

Among the most impressive *Atlantikwall* fortifications were two turrets from the battlecruiser *Gneisenau* emplaced in Norway at Örlandet and Fjell. The *Gneisenau* was damaged during the "Channel Dash" and while under repair, it was damaged again by an RAF raid. The subsequent reconstruction program planned to replace the existing triple 280mm SK C/28 in Drh L C/28 turrets with 380mm guns, freeing the weapons for coastal defense. The A turret had been damaged during an inconclusive duel with the HMS *Renown* during the April 1940 Norwegian campaign, and critically damaged in the February 26/27 RAF raid, so its guns were re-used in three new single turrets in Seezielbatterie Rozenburg in the Hook of Holland. In 1943, the B turret was disassembled and moved to Fjell while the C turret went to Örlandet. The Drh L C/28 turrets were modified in the process, with the stereoscopic rangefinders removed.

The Batterie Fjell was located on a rocky ridge on the island of Fjell about 175m above sea level, covering the southern approaches to Bergen. The 17m-deep shaft for the turret was excavated out of quartzite rock which minimized the need for extensive amounts of steel-reinforced concrete. Once completed, the turret was covered with the usual camouflage umbrella consisting of wooden outriggers and wire netting with painted metal squares and dried brush.

A large chamber was constructed under the gun turret for supporting equipment and ammunition. The chamber was connected to an extensive tunnel network, which linked the various supporting structures including an engine and generator chamber immediately behind the battery for power, a ventilator room, and a defensive bunker with 47mm anti-tank gun to protect the main entrance. There was also an ammunition reserve for about 300 rounds, connected

to the turret by a narrow gauge railway. The tunnels also led to an extensive underground gallery to the east of the turret containing the main crew quarters and additional ammunition storage. The S446 fire control post was located about 250m to the east, and could be reached by a tunnel. The complex was defended by several bunkers including two Bauform 633 with 50mm M19 automatic mortars, and a Bauform 629 antitank gun bunker. There was also a four-gun 88mm Flak battery near the site in concrete gun pits. Due to the importance of the battery, the fire control post was supported by a Freya surface search radar located to the east. The gun battery first underwent proof-firing in the summer of 1943, but never saw combat use.

The Fjell battery began to be disassembled in 1947 and completely scrapped by 1981; the turret shaft is now covered with a café. Its sister battery north of Trondheim, renamed Fort Austrat in Norwegian Kystartilleriet service, remained in service until finally decommissioned and converted into a museum with the turret still intact.

1. S446 command bunker
2. R633 bunker
3. Transformer bunker
4. Defense bunker
5. Crew quarters
6. Main entrance bunker
7. Main turret
8. Western access
A. Shell handling room
B. Charge handling room
C. Main ammunition trunk
D. Auxiliary ammunition hoist trunk

THE SITES TODAY

Belgium retains a number of coastal bunkers, and by the far the most interesting is Domain Raversijde on the western side of Ostend. This was the former royal domain that was turned over to the province of West Flanders by Prince Karel in 1981. Unlike other portions of the Belgian coast where the bunkers had been demolished, many bunkers remained intact on the estate. The park contains not only the extensive World War II Batterie Saltzwedel neu/Tirpitz, but also elements of the World War I Batterie Aachen. This is one of the most extensive and best-preserved sites on the entire *Atlantikwall* and contains numerous restored bunkers and gun positions. If I had to recommend a single *Atlantikwall* site for readers to visit, this would be the one.

The Netherlands was happy to rid itself of memories of the German occupation, and the severe flood of 1953 convinced the government to begin a campaign to remove most of the bunkers; their hasty construction and the risk of erosion posed a threat to the vital coastal dunes. Only a handful of large sites remain, although there are numerous bunkers scattered about. The concentration around IJmuiden is the most interesting as it includes the substantial Seezielbatterie Heerenduin in the dunes behind the parking lot of the seaside Holiday Inn along with some neighboring flak batteries. The IJmuiden Kernwerk is also nearby and can be visited on special tours. The corresponding battery site on the north side of the *Kernwerk* has disappeared under the massive Corus industrial park, but there are some batteries in neighboring Wijk-am-Zee. Another memorable site is Seezielbatterie Schveningen-Nord on the beach on the north side of the city. This battery is located in the protected coastal dunes and so is off limits, but can be easily seen from the beach. In contrast to the Amsterdam area, the extensive fortification efforts on the Hook of Holland near Rotterdam have largely been obliterated by the construction of the massive Europort dock facility, though there are still many scattered bunkers in the Nordmole area on the north side. The gun batteries involved in the violent battle for Walcheren have long since been removed, but the Bunkerbehoud foundation has been undertaking a program to restore some surviving personnel and observation bunkers in the area, including examples in Zoutelande and Vlissingen. These are little gems with extremely authentic reconstructions of the interior, which give a good idea of the wartime life in these bunkers.

Denmark took few pains to preserve the many bunkers along the western coast of Jutland, but in the 1980s the National Forest and Nature Agency began to catalog the surviving sites with an aim towards selecting some of the more significant sites for later preservation. In 2005, the Cultural Heritage Agency designated surviving bunkers to be "worthy of preservation," which obliges state agencies to consult before destroying surviving bunkers on state property; bunkers on private land are not protected. Many bunkers remain along the coast because they have proven to be too much trouble to remove.

Norway had relatively little heavy bunker construction considering the large number of gun batteries deployed there. After World War II, the Norwegien Kystartilleriet took over many of the better German gun batteries and kept them in service for many years. This preserved a number of batteries, but also limited public access as they became closed military posts. The most impressive are the Adolfkanonen at Trondenes and the Gneisenau turret at Orlandet; the Vara battery had its gun removed, but the large and incomplete gun casemate is still on site. There are large numbers of small German fortifications along the Norwegian coast including some rarities such as several PzKpfw II Flamingo *Panzerstellungen*.

For readers interested in visiting these sites, the books in the *Further reading* section that follows provide more detail, notably the regional studies. However, it is very helpful to check more recent information as access to many of these sites depends on the time of year. The Internet is a particularly useful source of information on the museums. In the case of some of the more remote bunkers which are not part of public museums, I have found that overhead topographic imagery such as that provided by Google Earth is enormously valuable in walking tours of the bunkers, especially when used in conjunction with GPS.

FURTHER READING

Although the history of the *Atlantikwall* in France is well covered in English language sources, this is not the case with the *Atlantikwall* in the Low Countries and Scandinavia, which has been largely ignored in English accounts. One of the better archival sources is the US Army's Seacoast Artillery Evaluation Board report, but copies are difficult to find except in the archives. I located examples at the National Archives and Records Administration (NARA II) in College Park, Maryland and the US Army Military History Institute at Carlisle Barracks, Pennsylvania. One of the strange aspects of this large study is that there is little coverage of France or the Low Countries, but relatively extensive detail on Scandinavia.

While there is little coverage of the *Atlantikwall* on the North Sea in English, there is abundant coverage in Flemish, Dutch, Danish, German, and Norwegian; some of the books listed below are multi-lingual with English or German sections. There is particularly good coverage of the Netherlands. Some of the regional studies are especially helpful if planning to visit the sites, as they often serve as catalogs of remaining fortifications.

UNPUBLISHED GOVERNMENT REPORTS
Clearing the Channel Ports: Part V Canadian Participation in the Operations in North-West Europe 1944. (Report No. 184, Historical Section, Canadian Military Headquarters)
German Seacoast Defenses – European Theater (7 volumes, Seacoast Artillery Evaluation Board, US Forces, ETO, 1945)

GENERAL *ATLANTIKWALL* STUDIES
Helmut Blocksdorf, *Hitler's Secret Commandos: Operations of the K-Verband* (Pen & Sword: 2008)
Lawrence Paterson, *Weapons of Desperation: German Frogmen and Midget Submarines of World War II* (Chatham: 2006)
Rudi Rolf, *Der Atlantikwall: Die Bauten der deutschen Küstenbefestigungen 1940–1945* (Zeller: 1998)
Rudi Rolf, *Der Atlantikwall: Perlenschnur aus Stahlbeton* (AMA: 1983)
Rudi Rolf, *Het Duitse Fortificatie-ontwerp 1935–1945* (Beetsterzwaag: 1985)
Rudi Rolf and Peter Saal, *Fortress Europe* (Airlife: 1988)
Hans Sakkers and Hans Houterman, *Atlantikwall in Zeeland en Vlaanderen* (Citadel: 2000)
Michael Schmeelke and Alarm Küste, *Deutsche Marine-, Heeres- und Luftwaffenbatterien in der Küstenverteidigung 1939–1945* (Dörfler: 2006)

BELGIUM

Alex Deseyne, *De Kust Bezet 1914–1918* (Goekink Graphics: 2007)

Alex Deseyne, *Raversijde 1914–1918: Geschiedenis van de Batterij Aachen* (West-Vlaanderen: 2005)

Frank Philippart et al, *De Atlantik Wall: Van Willemstad tot de Somme* (Lannoo: 2004)

Mariette Jacobs, *Raversijde 1940–1944: De Atlantikwall Batterij Saltzwedel neu/Tirpitz* (West-Vlaanderen: 1995)

Karl Schmeelke, Michael Schmeelke, *Deutsche Küstenbefestigungen in Belgien 1914–1945* (Podzun-Pallas: 1995)

Alain Van Geeteruvon, *De Atlanische Muur, Deel 1: De Bouwheren* (De Krijger, 1990)

Alain Van Geeteruvon and Dirk Peeters, *De Atlanische Muur, Deel 2: De Bunkers leger en marine types* (De Krijger, 1990)

DENMARK

Jens Andersen and Rudi Rolf, *German Bunkers in Denmark: A Survey* (PRAK: 2006)

Vibeke Ebert, *The Atlantic Wall from Nymindegab to Skallingen* (Blavandshuk Egnsmuseum: 1992)

M. Svejgaard, *The Kriegsmarine Command, Control and Reporting System, bunkers and electronic systems in Denmark 1940–45* (Gyges: 2007)

Peter Willumsen et al, *Der Atlantikwall auf Fano* (weXco: 2004)

THE NETHERLANDS

H.F. Ambachtsheer, *Van verdediging naar bescherming: De Atlantikwall in Den Haag* (VOM: 1995)

C. Bal, *Scheveningen-Den Haag 1940–1945: Van Dorp en Stad tot Stützpunktgruppe Scheveningen* (Rodi: 2001)

Peter Heijkoop and Jeroen Rijpsma, *De Atlantikwall op Goeree* (Rijpsma: 2006)

Maarten Peters, *De Atlantikwall: Omstreden erfgoed van Rijnmond tot IJmond* (Open Kaart: 2005)

Ruud Pols and Leo de Vries, *Seefront IJmuiden: Duitse bunkers in de kustverdediging van de Festung IJmuiden* (Pirola: 2005)

Jeroen Rijpsma and Klaas van Brakel, *Radarstellung Biber: Kustverdiging op Voorne 1940–45* (Rijpsma: 2005)

Rudi Rolf and Hans Sakkers, *Duitse bunkers in Nederland* (PRAK: 2005)

Hans Sakkers, *Festung Hoek van Holland* (Fortress Books: 1992)

Hans Sakkers, *Vesting Vlissingen* (Bunkerbehoud: 2004)

NORWAY

Roy Andersen, *Stride nom Strandsonen: Generalinspektoatet for Kystartilleriet 1899–2001* (Eide: 2005)

Trygve Dahl, *Festung Greipstad 1940–45* (Stiftelsen: 2005)

Erik Ettrup and Daniel Schellenberger, *Festung Lista: Atlanterhavsvollen i Norge* (Commentum: 2007)

Erik Ettrup, Erik Ritterbach and Daniel Schellenberger, *Der Atlantikwall in Norwegen: Festung Stavanger 1940–45* (Mails & More: 2005)

Jan Fjørtofy, *Tyske kystfort i Norge* (Agder: 1982)

Jan Olav Flatmark, *Sunnmøre i Festung Norwegen* (Snøhette: 1994)

Olav Kobbeltveit, *Fjell Festung i Krig og Fred* (Eide: 2006)

GLOSSARY

AOK	Armeeoberkommando; high command of an army
Art.Gr.	Artilleriegruppe, artillery group
Art.Ob.Gr.	Artillerieobergruppe, artillery super-group
Bauform	construction plan
E or EB	Eisenbahnbatterie: railroad battery
Festung	Fortress, major fortified area
Festungsbereich	fortified area
Flagruko	Flakgruppenkommandostand/stabsbatterie: flak group command post/staff battery
Flugplatz	Airbase
Heer	German Army
HKAA	Heeres-küsten-artillerie-abteilung, Army coastal artillery regiment
HKAR	Heeres-Küsten-artillerie-regiment, Army coastal artillery regiment
HKB	Heeresküstenbatterie; Army coastal battery
IR	Infantry regiment
K-Division	K-Verbände division
K-Flotilla	K-Verbände flotilla
Kernwerk	core position of Festung
KVA	Küsten Verteidigung Abschnitt, divisional coast defense sector
K-Verbände	also KdK, Kommando der Kleinkampfverbände, small combat unit command
Kriegsmarine	German Navy
KVG	Küsten Verteidigung Gruppe, coast defense group
Landfront	Fortified positions of coastal defense sector protecting rearward towards the land
MAA	Marine-artillerie-abteilung: Navy artillery regiment
Marko-Stand	Marineartilleriekommandostand/stabsbatterie: Naval artillery command post/staff battery
MEK	Marine Einsatz Kommando; commando units of the K-Verbände
MKB	Marine Küsten Batterie: Navy coastal battery
OB	offene Bettung, open platform
Regelbau	construction standard, sometimes abbreviated as R when used with a particular plan, for example R621
S-boat	German motor torpedo boat; often called E-boat by the Allies
Schartenstand	Gun casemate
Seeko	Seekommandant; regional naval command
Seezielbatterie	Naval battery; alternate of MKB
SK	bunker design suffix for Sonderkonstruktion, special design
St.P.	Stützpunkt; strongpoint, typically platoon to company size
St.P.Gr.	Stützpunktgruppe; strongpoint group, typically company to battalion size
Tobruk	A class of small bunkers with circular openings for a crew-served weapon
Tonne	Metric ton (1,000kg; 2.204 lb)
Unterstände	Bunker
VB	Verteidigungsbereich; defense zone
Vf	Verstarkfeldmässig; reinforced field position such as a tobruk
W or WN	Widerstandsnest; resistance nest, typically section to platoon sized
Westwall	German fortifications created in the late 1930s on the French–German border, also known as Siegfried Line

INDEX